Service Level Agreements

A legal and practical guide

GW00645037

Service Level Agreements

A legal and practical guide

JIMMY DESAI

IT Governance Publishing

Every possible effort has been made to ensure that the information contained in this book is accurate at the time of going to press, and the publishers and the author cannot accept responsibility for any errors or omissions, however caused. No responsibility for loss or damage occasioned to any person acting, or refraining from action, as a result of the material in this publication can be accepted by the publisher or the author.

Apart from any fair dealing for the purposes of research or private study, or criticism or review, as permitted under the Copyright, Designs and Patents Act 1988, this publication may only be reproduced, stored or transmitted, in any form, or by any means, with the prior permission in writing of the publisher or, in the case of reprographic reproduction, in accordance with the terms of licences issued by the Copyright Licensing Agency. Enquiries concerning reproduction outside those terms should be sent to the publishers at the following address:

IT Governance Publishing
IT Governance Limited
Unit 3, Clive Court
Bartholomew's Walk
Cambridgeshire Business Park
Ely
Cambridgeshire
CB7 4EH
United Kingdom

www.itgovernance.co.uk

The author has asserted the rights of the author under the Copyright, Designs and Patents Act, 1988, to be identified as the author of this work.

First published in the United Kingdom in 2010 by
IT Governance Publishing.

ISBN 978-1-84928-069-3

FOREWORD

This pocket guide has been written with the following readers in mind, although others should also find the information useful:

- Chief executive officers
- Managing directors
- Finance directors
- Strategic directors
- Senior management teams
- IT and outsourcing lawyers (both in private practice and in house)
- Chief information officers and IT directors
- IT procurement professionals
- Service level and contract managers
- IT and process consultants
- IT managers
- Technical service managers
- Service delivery managers
- Client service relationship managers
- Help desk analysts
- Network support engineers
- IT sales professionals.

A wide range of industry sectors will outsource service provision (for example, banking, pharmaceuticals, travel and insurance companies). This can happen where an organisation outsources its IT payroll needs, its helpdesk and IT maintenance requirements, its payment processing, or its whole IT function.

Foreword

A key aspect of any such outsourcing is the standard of service that is given by the service provider. This standard of service is often governed by an SLA (service level agreement).

This pocket guide identifies some of the benefits and the pitfalls that an organisation can encounter when negotiating and drafting SLAs.

PREFACE

The idea for this pocket guide came about because numerous organisations were regularly encountering and seeking advice upon the same, or similar, legal and practical issues surrounding SLAs.

Many of the issues that they were facing were not new. However, organisations were spending a lot of management time, effort and costs in deciphering SLA issues for themselves.

This time, effort and money could have been used to consider and solve more novel issues relating to SLAs and outsourcing arrangements, rather than being spent on issues which were commonplace in the industry, and for which tried and tested solutions already existed.

The information in this pocket guide provides an overview of SLAs, highlighting typical scenarios that can arise, and providing information on typical solutions that have been adopted by other organisations.

By providing a short, legal and practical guide to SLAs, the reader should be able to quickly come up to speed with some of the legal and practical issues that might arise. The idea of this pocket guide is that it is short and easy to digest, and as such it does not attempt to cover every issue or element that can arise within an SLA. Case references and weblinks have been provided in the text where readers can find more information about SLAs.

ABOUT THE AUTHOR

Jimmy Desai is a partner at law firm Beachcroft LLP, in the City of London, and has been advising upon, formulating and implementing SLA contracts and strategies, benefits and cost savings for businesses, since the mid 1990s. Throughout his career he has advised major international blue- chip companies, governments, industry bodies, IT customers and suppliers on their service level agreements.

He writes extensively for a wide range of IT publications, and lectures at international conferences, both in the UK and abroad. He has lectured at the University of London and the University of Stirling and, as well as a law degree, he has a Masters Degree (First Class) in Electronic Engineering and postgraduate qualifications in Intellectual Property Law and Practice.

Jimmy is a member of TIPLO (The Intellectual Property Lawyers Organisation), ITMA (The Institute of Trade Mark Agents), SCL (The Society for Computers and Law), EuroITcounsel, Intellect (an IT trade body), and ITechLaw.

Jimmy is listed as one of the top 40 Internet and e-commerce lawyers in the UK in the International Who's Who of Internet and E-Commerce Lawyers 2010.

ACKNOWLEDGEMENTS

This is my second pocket guide for IT Governance Ltd and has been written whilst working as a lawyer in the City of London, where I advise numerous clients on their legal needs and strategies regarding SLAs, so that they can obtain better and more cost-effective services.

It could not have been written without the support and assistance of my colleagues, a very understanding and patient publisher in the form of Angela Wilde at IT Governance Ltd, and the support of friends, family, clients and reviewers when talking about the ideas and principles involved in this pocket guide.

I am also grateful for the patience, support and input of my wife, Sarah Hanchet.

CONTENTS

CHAPTER 1: WHY DO YOU NEED A SERVICE LEVEL AGREEMENT?

It is true to say that many organisations look at outsourcing (including IT outsourcing) to cut costs. Some organisations look to outsource for other reasons, such as streamlining their businesses, or re-organising the way that they do business. Although organisations are often interested in cutting costs via outsourcing, they do not want this to mean that the standard of service falls. In fact, many organisations want to obtain the best of both worlds, by cutting costs via outsourcing, but also obtaining better services than they received previously.

References in this pocket guide to 'you', 'your' and 'your organisation', are a reference to a customer organisation that wishes to outsource the provision of certain services to a supplier and, as such, needs to enter into an SLA in order to ensure that it receives the services commissioned to pre- agreed standards.

Key risks for an organisation that enters into an outsourcing transaction, are that the services that it receives from the supplier will be worse than the services they were receiving before, or that the cost savings that were anticipated or promised, are not achieved.

To try to avoid this scenario, the outsourcing contract should include a service level agreement (SLA). This SLA must be drafted so that the services and associated standards of service that you require are absolutely clear, including the cost of those services and the consequences of not achieving pre-agreed standards.

In order to be able to produce an SLA that suits your requirements, you must have a good understanding of the kind of services that your organisation is currently receiving (and their standards and cost). By understanding the services you currently receive, you can better explain what you need to a new supplier and ensure that the services you obtain are at least as good as those you had in place previously. You will also be able to compare the cost of any current services with any proposed new services.

Even if the price is right and the legal provisions provide enough legal protection for your organisation in the event of various breaches (e.g. breaches of IP rights, breaches of confidentiality, etc.), this is not really a satisfactory substitute for poor service. In other words, although the legal issues in the outsourcing deal documentation are important, it is the service that your organisation will notice (particularly if the service is poor), and it is often the service itself that will generally dictate whether or not your organisation is happy with the overall deal.

When negotiating any type of service-related deal (including any IT outsourcing deal), it is essential that sufficient time is devoted to ensuring that the service is of sufficient quality and that this is recorded in a service level agreement (SLA), rather than the SLA being an afterthought.

The way that an IT outsourcing deal is normally

structured in a legal context, and in a legal document, is by having a framework agreement (sometimes called a 'master agreement' or 'umbrella agreement') which contains primarily commercial and legal terms (e.g. price, length of the contract, break provisions, intellectual property, and the law by which the IT outsourcing deal is to be governed, etc.). The detailed description of the services and their quality, quantity, standards and delivery timetables, etc. is usually included in an appendix, or schedule to the framework agreement, in the form of an SLA. The framework agreement and its schedules or appendices (including the SLA), is often referred to, as a whole, as the 'IT outsourcing contract', the 'outsourcing contract', the 'master services contract' or the 'services contract'.

The broad principles in this pocket guide can be adopted for SLAs both between your organisation and external third parties or, alternatively, between different business units in your own organisation.

One key difference between an SLA between you and a third party, compared to an SLA between different business units in your own organisation, is that SLAs with third parties tend to be drafted in a way that is legally enforceable (and where the parties to it might seek to enforce it legally in the courts). Internal SLAs will tend to be more informal documents.

Other reasons why you might need SLAs include:

- **Influencing supplier behaviour**: SLAs can influence supplier behaviour and focus the supplier's mind on things which are important to your organisation. For example, providing bonuses and incentives can influence the supplier in terms of where it devotes its time, energies and attention. Also, if there are penalties (often referred to as credits) payable to the customer if certain elements of a service are provided to a poor standard, this can act as a deterrent against the supplier providing a poor service.

- **Defining or explaining the service and the required standard of service**: some people (including some suppliers) may think that all organisations are interested in achieving a 'standard' service and so will want the same services, service levels and targets – however, this is often not the case since 'one size does not fit all'.

Many organisations may have specific issues regarding the services they need from their supplier (which are particular to them, based on their business model, industry sector, or client requirements, etc.), and so the SLA will need to reflect these specific issues.

For example, this can happen where:

- Your organisation is subject to the rules and regulations of particular regulatory bodies (e.g. the Financial Services Authority or other financial regulatory bodies), such that the way that you operate your business is monitored and scrutinised by such external bodies.
- Your organisation works in a fast-moving environment (e.g. share trading, where IT resolutions for IT systems are required almost immediately).

- Your organisation has promised to meet certain deadlines with clients (and this is efficiently and without long down times).

Do you actually need an SLA?

It is important to consider whether or not you actually need an SLA in the first place.

In some cases an SLA may not be required (or may only be required in a short, basic form), because the cost, time and effort in actually creating the SLA, is many times larger than the total deal value. In this case it might not make commercial or economic sense to have a detailed SLA.

In some deals an SLA is required (and should have been incorporated into the deal documentation) but the parties have simply forgotten to incorporate it, have overlooked the need for it altogether, or simply did not know that an SLA might be needed.

However, organisations that overlook or forget to use an SLA where vital services are being procured, can find that because the quality and standard of the services was not pre-agreed, there can be a dispute later on about what the quality and standard of these services should have been.

In some cases an SLA may not be needed because it does not fit in with the deal structure (see the following scenarios):

1. Where the services to be provided are over a very short duration (e.g. a day or a week), which does

not give enough time to measure them, and also creates a cost and administrative burden on an which will only be in place for a short period of time.

2. Where the services being provided are 'one off' (rather than being ongoing) and are only paid for when they have been delivered to a satisfactory standard (i.e. if services are only paid for once certain milestones have been achieved). This might happen in projects such as software development, when payment is only made when certain deliverables have been achieved, delivered and accepted by your organisation (such that it is the output of the activity that is paid for, rather than monitoring how the activity is actually performed).

3. Where it is only goods that are being provided (rather than any services). For example, where computer equipment is simply being purchased by your organisation and where no services are being procured.

Note that in the above scenarios, although a full SLA may not be used, there will be other types of agreement that will govern the relationship between your organisation and the supplier. For example, in (3) above, where computer equipment is being purchased, then this may be implemented by a sale and purchase agreement (which covers issues such as equipment to be provided, specification, price and delivery date, etc.) such that no ongoing SLA is required. However, if, for example, maintenance services or helpdesk services, etc. are going to be provided with the computer equipment, then an SLA might be required.

1: Why do you Need a Service Level Agreement?

Typically, SLAs will be in place for various IT maintenance, helpdesk, support, capacity, availability and hosting obligations, or where the services to be provided are:

- long term
- high value
- complex
- business critical.

Document structure

A frequently asked question is 'Where does the SLA document fit into the deal documentation as a whole?'

Typically, there will be a framework agreement which will refer to 'the services' as a defined term in that agreement.

As mentioned above, the SLA (being specifically to do with services and service standards), will often be contained in a schedule, or appendix, to the framework agreement. It is also important to note that the framework agreement, together with all of its schedules and/or appendices (including the SLA), is – as mentioned above – sometimes referred to as a whole as the 'IT outsourcing contract', the 'outsourcing contract', the 'master services contract' or the 'services contract'.

Having a structured framework agreement with a schedule containing the SLA has advantages because the key legal terms for the overall deal (in the framework agreement) are separated from specific deliverables, technical details and timetables, which relate to the services that appear in the SLA.

This means that specific service details in the SLA are not mixed up, and are separated from, legal clauses, such as limitations of liability, indemnities, intellectual property, exclusion clauses and data protection clauses, etc. so there is a clear delineation between legal terms and practical details about services.

The SLA can encompass and focus upon services, technical information and service standards.

People at your organisation that understand the specific and practical service details of what is required (e.g. CIOs, IT directors and IT managers), can focus time on the SLA, whereas other people at your organisation (e.g. CEOs, managing directors, finance directors, lawyers, etc.) can focus more of their time on the framework agreement and the commercial and legal terms contained within it. These personnel will need to liaise with one another, since the framework agreement and SLA need to tie into one another, but this separation between where the legal terms are covered (in the framework agreement), and the practical description and way in which the services are to be implemented (in the SLA), can help to make the negotiation and preparation process more efficient and streamlined.

Another benefit of this approach is that any person interested in, and responsible for, monitoring and managing services (such as project managers), can easily refer to the SLA, without having to always read all of the legal terms in the framework agreement. This is useful where legal terms in framework agreements covering larger deals can contain numerous documents and can, in some cases, run to hundreds of pages, not all of which will impact upon the day-to-day service provision under the SLA.

The SLA is a 'living, breathing document', in that it is likely to change from time to time, depending upon what services are required, and an organisation's changing business needs. It is likely that the SLA will change far more often than the framework agreement.

Hence, if services need to be amended, then by having the services catered for in the SLA, they can be changed by simply amending the SLA, without having to change all of the framework agreement documentation that relates to the deal.

Some people talk about SLAs as being a 'stand- alone' document. However, although it is useful to separate SLAs from the framework agreement for the reasons above, the SLA is normally part of it (as it is normally included as a schedule or appendix).

Note that there will also be other schedules or appendices to the framework agreement, as well as the SLA. In an outsourcing transaction, your organisation may, as part of the deal, transfer assets to the supplier, for the supplier to operate the services. These assets may include some of your organisation's existing IT systems and/or related computer equipment. In any cvent, if assets are to be transferred from your organisation to the supplier as part of the deal, then there would be a schedule to the framework agreement which lists those assets to be transferred and details about them (e.g. price, condition, or any other relevant information). Other schedules or appendices to the framework agreement might include issues, such as:

1. Employees who are transferring from your organisation to the supplier as part of the outsourcing deal.
2. Disaster recovery plans.
3. Exit plans to cater for what happens at the end of the IT deal, in terms of how the IT supplier handles the transfer of its services back to your organisation, or your organisation's replacement supplier.
4. Any contracts relating to your organisation's IT with any third parties which are to be transferred to the IT supplier, so it can manage them on your organisation's behalf.

The point here is that, as mentioned above, the framework agreement often covers the overarching commercial and legal terms relating to the deal. However, the SLA (covering service standards, etc.), together with issues such as those in (1) – (4) above (inclusive), are dealt with in different schedules or appendices to the framework agreement, so as to focus upon those separate issues, without mixing them up with legal and commercial terms in the framework agreement.

For example, the framework agreement might say that:

- The deal is to last for two years.
- The price is £1,000,000.
- All IP created is to belong to your organisation.
- Your organisation can terminate the deal at any time, upon six months notice to the supplier.

- There are various exclusions and limitations.
- The deal is governed by English law.

This is known as 'deal information'. Having this 'deal information' in the framework agreement, means that it covers all of the aspects in each of the schedules or appendices to the framework agreement, so that it does not have to be repeated and duplicated in each schedule or appendix.

Each schedule or appendix will be cross- referenced to the framework agreement, so as to streamline the overall document structure. For example, the 'disaster recovery plan' might be referred to in the framework agreement, but each reference to this will direct the reader to the relevant schedule of the framework agreement, to find out more about the details of disaster recovery. The same principle applies regarding the SLA, which will be defined in the framework agreement, but then the reader will be referred to the relevant schedule of the framework agreement which contains the SLA, in order to find out more about the services and service standards being provided.

Service levels and service level targets

Before entering into an SLA, there are some key questions that need to be answered by your organisation, which include:

- What services or outputs do you require (the 'service')?
- What are you going to choose as a measure of

those services (often referred to as the 'service level')?

- What is the percentage target that is required to achieve the requisite standard (often referred to as 'the service level target')?
- How much compensation is payable if the required target is not met (often referred to as 'the service level credit')?

In practice, your organisation may outsource all of its IT department requirements to a third party supplier. Questions that might arise, include:

- What services do you require (e.g. telephone helpdesk services, to assist users when they have problems with their computers)?
- What is the measure, standard or yard stick, of how good such a telephone helpdesk service actually is? Is this how quickly the call is responded to, i.e. within four telephone rings? How quickly a workaround is found so that the user can continue to work? How quickly a total fix is found? What will the chosen service level be?
- How often must the agreed service target be met (e.g. an answer within four telephone rings)? Will this standard being met 99% of the time be sufficient? What is the service level target going to be?
- How much compensation is payable for a breach (e.g. is £x payable for every ring over and above four rings, where the telephone is not answered)? (i.e. what is the service level credit going to be?).

There are some other issues which relate to the

examples above, including:

- If the service level is, say, the telephone being answered within four rings, then will a user being answered by computer generated call options be sufficient to satisfy this standard (i.e. if a user is faced with an automated voice answering system which responds within four rings by saying, 'press one for hardware problems, press two for software problems and press three for other problems', will this suffice?)?
- Over what period is the 99% service level target measured (is it a day, a week, a month, or a quarter, or some other period)? This timing could affect supplier behaviour because if compensation is payable immediately for a fault (without the supplier having time to resolve the issue), then it might mean that the supplier may not put as much energy into resolving the problem, compared to the situation in which no compensation is payable if the fault is resolved within a fixed period of time.
- What happens if the 99% service level target is not met? Is monetary compensation enough (and is this actually what your organisation wants), or does your organisation want action to resolve the problem, as an alternative to, or in addition to, monetary compensation?
- If compensation is required, then at what level should it be set? In the example above, what if the phone was answered in five rings (i.e. one ring late)? Is this really deserving of compensation? The answer is 'probably not', but then where does an organisation draw the line at where and when compensation (i.e. service level credits) should be

payable? In this example, perhaps no one answering the phone after 15 rings might cause enough disruption, so that if this happens all the time, then it is deserving of compensation to your organisation. This scenario then points towards some kind of grace period, or allowance (i.e. that any response made before 15 rings attracts no service credits, but any response at 15 rings, or above, attracts a service credit).

For example, if the phone is picked up within four rings, then this meets the target (no compensation payable). If the phone is not picked up in five-15 rings, then this is a breach which must be resolved, but no compensation is payable. If the phone is picked up in 15+ rings, then the problem must be resolved and compensation is also payable by way of service credits.

This is a simple example, but it is used to demonstrate some principles regarding SLAs, which are that:

- The organisation's desire is that it wants quick response times when it calls a telephone helpdesk, so that it is not waiting around for a response, or does not receive any response at all. However, having identified that this is the desired outcome, this is broken down in to a formula (e.g. calls answered within a number of rings).
- The measurements which are made should be objective and measurable (rather than subjective targets which are difficult to measure).
- Your organisation will need to carefully consider the matrix of exactly what service outputs it requires, and then translate these into services,

service levels, targets and credits, that accurately reflect what it requires.

This process of understanding, codifying and translating your organisation's requirements and desired service outputs and outcomes into objective service levels and targets, can be a challenging and time-consuming exercise.

However, it is a good idea to approach the preparation of the SLA in this way, compared to your organisation automatically signing up to a standard untailored SLA that might be tabled by the supplier, and which does not reflect your organisation's particular requirements or desired outcomes or outputs.

Breach of service level targets – compensation and action plans

As explained above, a service level target of 99% might be breached. Your organisation will need to look at what remedy is required should this occur.

Compensation, or service credits (which some people might refer to as 'penalties'), are often inserted into an SLA. This is not because the customer's primary aim is to get compensation or service credits, since monetary compensation may be paid long after the breach of service and does not provide the customer with any real remedy at the time that the breach occurs (i.e. compensation does not mean that poor service will be remedied at the time it occurs). For example, if computers are meant to have an uptime of 99% each week, but fall below this to 95% availability in a week, then the customer has suffered poor service and possible business disruption during that week. However, compensation payable later on regarding this breach, may be of little comfort to the customer (as what they would have preferred is for the uptime of 99% to have been met and for their business to have not been disrupted in the first place).

Hence, compensation or service credits are usually inserted into an SLA to act as a deterrent, so that the supplier does not breach service levels, otherwise they will have to pay compensation or service credits (and the supplier will not want to do this, as this will reduce its profits).

Service credits may seem a good way of ensuring breaches do not happen, but this may not always be the case. For example, this compensation may have already been factored into the supplier's pricing, so that even if the supplier does pay compensation, it is still likely to make a healthy profit.

Hence, it might be more effective for an organisation to demand that, as well as compensation, problems are fixed within a certain period of time, and that the supplier is obliged to dedicate certain personnel and resources to fixing the problem. In this case, there could be an action plan which is set out in the SLA, regarding what is to happen if and when service levels fall below pre-agreed levels. Action plans can be useful because this means that:

- Your organisation can at least be assured that something is being done about the problem, rather than just simply receiving compensation without a

satisfactory resolution to the problem.
- The supplier is clear about what action it needs to take, if and when, services fall below pre- agreed standards.

Your organisation may also allow the supplier to earn back credits (*as mentioned in Chapter 4*), as an incentive to resolve problems as soon as possible.

Advantages of defining remedies

One major advantage with SLAs, and why you might want an SLA in place, is because there are pre-defined remedies for breaches of service level targets.

This is particularly useful because an organisation does not want to incur the time, effort and expense of suing a supplier in court for relatively small breaches of the service levels. This is because with small breaches of the service levels:

- The cost of going to court is likely to outweigh the cost of how much your organisation has lost as a result of the breach.
- Taking legal action against a supplier is likely to signal the end of the relationship (where your organisation may actually be dependent upon the supplier for all, or most, of your IT requirements).
- There is no guarantee that your organisation will win in court, since a supplier may blame, or ascribe, lapses or defaults by your organisation as causing the supplier's default.
- Whilst court action is ongoing, your organisation may still have to continue working with a supplier

that is demotivated or uncooperative, or your organisation might have to find an alternative supplier in a hurry (which will probably mean that your organisation incurs further costs).

Using pre-defined remedies can help your organisation and supplier maintain their relationship because your organisation can implement certain pre-agreed remedies if the supplier does not provide the service levels to the agreed service level targets. However, service level credits (which are usually designed for day-to-day breaches of service quality) are unlikely to be sufficient to compensate your organisation for major breaches regarding service standards (where such major breaches have a huge impact on the IT deal as a whole).

Major breaches

It is important to note that SLAs tend to cater for relatively minor day-to-day breaches of pre-agreed service level targets, where some compensation and/or an action plan will resolve the issue. SLAs are not usually designed to cater for major and substantial breaches of IT outsourcing deals as a whole. The rights and remedies regarding major breaches are usually catered for in the framework agreement, although breaches of the SLA can be taken into account when taking action for major breaches under the terms of the framework agreement.

For example, there may be a service level target to say that an engineer from the supplier will arrive on your organisation's site to fix problems within four hours of being given notice to do so. There may be compensation payable for every hour that they are late (e.g. £100 for every hour over four hours during a working that the engineer does not turn up). However, if your organisation's whole IT system fails and an engineer does not turn up for five days (e.g. around 25 working hours after they were called), then will £2,500 be sufficient compensation? Probably not, if your organisation has suffered major losses (e.g. £500,000), due to the IT being inoperable for such a long period of time. Any legal action might be taken primarily with reference to the framework agreement.

Therefore, although an SLA can provide pre- agreed compensation and/or an action plan for relatively minor breaches, your organisation should not be tied to the SLA so that it has no other options for redress. Hence, your organisation should be at liberty to pursue any other action, such as court action against a supplier, if your organisation believes that the standard of service is so poor that the SLA provisions are not enough to compensate it sufficiently.

This is mentioned because some SLAs state that the pre-agreed amounts of compensation and/or action plans are your organisation's 'sole and exclusive remedy'. If your organisation wants the option to pursue the supplier in court via the framework agreement or otherwise (and regardless of what the SLA provides for), then your organisation should not agree to such limitations on its rights of redress.

In other words, the SLA should be an option for your organisation to obtain remedies, but it should not be the only option. Your organisation should have the option to look for greater remedies and compensation (over and above those contained in the SLA) if there is a major breach, or a breach which causes substantial losses. Your organisation's other rights of redress may be contained in the framework agreement, or under general legal principles.

Fairness

When agreeing an SLA with a supplier, your organisation should strive to ensure that the SLA is fair and balanced, and has the full buy-in and support of your organisation and the supplier.

The SLA is primarily an operational document that governs day-to-day service issues. Because of the nature of the SLA, it should not have lots of legal carve outs, provisos, pre-conditions and complex clauses because it is going to be operated and implemented by project personnel (and not the parties' respective lawyers).

The SLA is also likely to change, or be updated regularly, during the course of the deal, as your organisation's business develops and grows over time (meaning that your organisation's service requirements change over time).

Although it is clear that your organisation should not negotiate an SLA so that it is to its detriment, it should also not swing to the other side, where the SLA is all 'one way' and all in your organisation's favour.

The reason for this is that creating a fair and balanced SLA is likely to build trust and co- operation between the parties, including their full buy-in and support, whereas an unfair and unbalanced

1: Why do you Need a Service Level Agreement?

SLA is simply likely to lead to problems and disputes.

Clauses which your organisation could insert, but which would tend to make the SLA unfair and unbalanced, include things such as:

- Service credits being so high that they could eat into all of the profit that the supplier might make from the relevant period, or even lead to the supplier making a loss for the relevant period.
- The supplier having to provide a lot of services for no charge at all.
- The supplier having to compete with other suppliers for every new piece of work that relates to your IT systems.

The problems that your organisation can face if it has an SLA which is all in its favour (and which does not have the full support or buy-in of the supplier) include:

- The supplier losing interest in your service provision and therefore doing the bare minimum.
- The supplier looking to more lucrative contracts (and spending more time on those, and assigning its best people to those other contracts, rather than your issues).
- The supplier taking 'short cuts' in order to save time, money and resources (since the spending of that time, money and resources on dealing with your organisation's issues might, in the supplier's opinion, make the SLA economically unviable).
- The supplier trying to charge for services which are not mentioned in the SLA, but which your organisation might have thought were already

covered and included in the agreed services (and associated price).T
- he supplier not strictly complying with the pre-defined service levels, targets and credits, but it being too expensive, time-consuming or inconvenient for your organisation to enforce these provisions via the courts.

Although in a tough economic climate your organisation may be able to negotiate an SLA with a supplier which is all in your organisation's favour (perhaps because the supplier is keen to secure the work and obtain the business), your organisation may find that if it abuses its good bargaining position, or has unrealistic expectations, then this could lead to some of the problems above.

Other reasons why you need SLAs

SLAs can assist your organisation and a supplier because they allow each party to be specific about their respective expectations regarding the rights and responsibilities of the other party. This can be in the form of describing:

- The services that are to be provided and the required standards.
- The services that will not be provided, or which will be treated as being extra and therefore cost more.
- The system and/or structure which the supplier expects your organisation to have in place before it begins work. For example, a supplier might need your organisation to have a computer system of a particular specification in place, and in working order, before it can provide its goods and/or

services. Failure to have this in place will then not be taken into account if the supplier cannot provide its goods and services because you do not have the right system in place.

- Explaining how much, or the basis for charging, regarding any additional services required by your organisation (e.g. this might be hourly rates for services provided, a level of travel and accommodation expenses, and also any other costs and expenses which the supplier would want to charge for).

- Placing obligations upon your organisation regarding service defaults (i.e. your organisation may be obliged to report problems as soon as possible; to co-operate with, and follow, the reasonable instructions of the supplier; and provide access to equipment to supplier personnel, regarding any resolution activities). Any failure by your organisation to comply with its obligations here could then mean that the relevant service level targets may not apply, and any associated service credits may be reduced or may not be payable at all.

- Allowing for periods which are not taken into account when calculating whether service level targets have been met (i.e. a supplier will generally require that any scheduled down time for regular maintenance or upgrade work will not be counted in any uptime target calculation).

- When service level target breaches are not eligible for service credit breaches. For example, if your organisation specifically wants the computer system to be upgraded, then any down time for any upgrade work to take place, will not count against the supplier, and will not be taken into account in any uptime target calculation (or any calculation of service level credits).

- What you believe to be within the capability of the supplier. Simply working on the SLA with the supplier can help you assess whether or not the supplier is over promising, regarding what it can provide. See the Sky v EDS[1] case which, amongst other things, shows that a supplier which 'over promises' on what it can provide, can not only cause problems for the supplier, but also the customer (whereby the customer has business disruption, and also has the task of taking the supplier to court, with all of the time, cost and effort that this process entails). A lesson from this case is that the customer should also consider double checking with the supplier as to whether or not they can, indeed, provide the relevant services and service standards required in the relevant timescales set out in the SLA (rather than the customer simply relying solely upon all of the information provided by one person at the supplier where, if the customer had double checked, might have turned out not to all be accurate).

If the supplier has agreed to service levels and targets in the SLA, then your organisation will have a claim against the supplier if these are not met. However, in order to avoid such situations, it is important for your organisation and the supplier to discuss these service levels and targets in detail, so that they are set at

---

[1] BSkyB Limited (and others) v HP Enterprise Services UK Limited (formerly EDS Limited) [2010] EWHC 86 (TCC).

realistic levels which are likely to be delivered successfully.

Summary

In summary, before entering into an SLA your organisation will need to understand:

- Whether or not you actually need an SLA.
- How the SLA will fit into the overall document structure which covers the deal.
- The services which it needs (broken down in detail and setting out standards that are required, via service levels and service level targets).
- Remedial action that is required if services do not meet pre-agreed standards.
- Areas where service levels, service level targets, and service level credits, will not apply, such as in the case of major breaches of contract.
- What each party's detailed expectations are, in terms of the services to be provided and service standards. The next chapter explains some of the reasons why SLAs can go wrong.

CHAPTER 2: WHERE SLAS GO WRONG

Legal protection

Under general law[2], if services are to be provided to an organisation by a supplier, they must be provided with 'reasonable skill and care', and goods provided must be of 'satisfactory quality'.

In terms of 'reasonable skill and care', this could be described as the standard of skill and care that would normally be expected of someone in that particular field.

'Satisfactory quality' means that the goods should meet the standard a reasonable person would regard as satisfactory, taking into account the description of the goods, the price (if relevant) and all other relevant circumstances. The quality of the goods includes their state and condition, including their appearance and finish, freedom from minor defects, safety and durability. They should also be fit for all purposes for which goods of that kind are commonly supplied.

The general law which governs the purchase of goods and services often applies more to consumer transactions. However, businesses (e.g. an IT business customer and an IT supplier) usually have written and negotiated contracts between themselves, rather than relying upon general law to determine the standards of services to be provided, the price, and all other

---

2 See the Supply of Goods and Services Act 1982 and the Sale of Goods Act 1979 (as amended by The Sale and Supply of Goods Act 1994 and The Sale and Supply of Goods to Consumers Regulations 2002).

circumstances relating to the provision of services and their use.

In other words, without an SLA, if IT goods and services are provided to a poor standard by the supplier under an outsourcing contract, then a customer would have to argue in court that the IT services (which could be a vast array of services costing millions of pounds and providing in numerous ways at different sites) were not being provided with reasonable skill and care, and/or that the goods provided were not of satisfactory quality.

Any such claims under general law (where a framework agreement and SLA are not in place) might be strongly resisted and defended by a supplier, particularly where the supplier can provide plausible or valid arguments as to why:

- The goods are of satisfactory quality (or a large proportion of them are).
- The services have been provided with reasonable skill and care (or a large proportion of the services are provided with reasonable skill and care).
- The goods or services would have been provided correctly were it not for the defaults or wrong doing of the customer.

As can be seen here, it could become quite difficult for a customer to get a satisfactory remedy because of all of the obstacles that a supplier might put in the way of any claim by a customer, if a framework agreement and/or SLA is not in place. Having an SLA means that the services can be broken down into segments and clearly defined, so that it becomes much more difficult for a supplier to argue that it is not in breach of certain agreed service levels and standards. Because of this, SLAs help to provide written certainty and granularity regarding services to be provided, for both the customer and the supplier.

An important point to remember is that the service levels and service level targets are often chosen, so that if all of these are met, then you should obtain a good service. Because of this, the temptation is to choose numerous service levels and service level targets, in order to make sure that everything is covered, regarding every element of service provision.

However, the danger with this approach is that the SLA can then go wrong because it loses focus, is difficult to monitor and manage, and also if you miss out any particular service level, then the supplier may argue that it could be implied that this missed out point is not covered and/or is not important. Hence, it could be that less is more here (in that fewer, more targeted service levels and targets, are actually more useful in practice than hundreds of service levels and targets).

Changes

SLAs usually cover long-term service provision. However, your organisation may be taken over, may merge with another organisation, or may need to increase or reduce the services required. The SLA can then go wrong because it is drafted at a specific point in time and has not been drafted in a way which caters for possible future changes in your organisation's service requirements.

For example, an organisation with a five-year contract with an IT supplier, recently decided to merge with a similar organisation. However, the other organisation already had a different IT supplier. Upon merger of the organisations, it did not make sense to have two IT suppliers (who were, in fact, competitors) providing very similar IT services. The newly merged organisation would ideally have liked to select one IT supplier to provide all of its IT services. Because of this, it was fortunate that one of the organisations had provisions in its contract which allowed it to reduce, or cancel, services from its IT supplier, if that organisation ever merged. This provision was invoked by the newly merged organisation, in order to allow them to have one IT supplier provide the IT services which it required.

Because of situations like the above, it is important to try to 'future proof' your framework agreement and SLA, by:

- Including provisions to cover foreseeable events or circumstances (so that if such events or circumstances occur, then it is clear what should happen).
- Including a change procedure in the SLA, so that if your organisation, or the IT supplier, wants to change anything to do with the services, then there is a formal route and procedure for doing so.
-

Any change procedure can also specify the timescales which the parties need to respond to one another, regarding any change requests; the type of information that each party should provide to the other, regarding any change request; any payment to the IT supplier for carrying out any scoping work, regarding the change required; and also the rates, or basis upon which, the IT supplier will implement any changes.

In your SLA, your organisation may also try to negotiate that it obtains a certain number of free changes (provided that these do not take more than a certain number of man days) per year, so that your organisation at least knows that it can make a limited number of changes to the service free of charge. Free changes might include that you want different reports to be provided to you in place of, or in addition to, the reports which your organisation originally specified, just because, as the deal progressed, your organisation became aware that it required different types of information, or more detailed information via reports.

Including a change procedure in your SLA will assist your organisation, and the IT supplier, in managing any changes (whether expected or unexpected), and therefore avoid disputes or any legal action regarding any such changes (such as disputes over the timing, cost, or number of changes).

Lawyers can help you avoid any disputes by drafting the correct change procedures into your SLA.

Who prepares the SLA?

The SLA can go wrong from the very start because it is prepared and negotiated by the wrong people at your organisation, or by people at your organisation (or your organisation's external advisors or consultants) who do not fully understand the services and service standards that your organisation requires, or what your organisation is trying to achieve. Hence, the SLA can accurately reflect those people's views of what your organisation was trying to achieve, but this may not actually tally with the exact desired services, outputs and outcomes of your organisation.

SLAs can go wrong because the customer and/or the supplier might sometimes:

- Try to hand over all responsibility regarding preparation and negotiation of the SLA to their respective lawyers (where these lawyers may not have all the background information about what is actually required by your organisation, in terms of scope of services and associated standards).
- Try to handle all of the SLA documentation themselves, and having created and finalised it, just ask lawyers to do a final 'check' of the SLA. However, this 'check' is often after negotiations have finished, so that there is no real opportunity to make changes to the SLA (even if problems are spotted, since trying to address these problems might then re-open negotiations, which might, in turn, delay or jeopardise the whole deal).
- Rely on a so-called 'standard' SLA (which might be produced by the supplier), which is signed just to 'tick the box', so that the parties can say that there is some kind of SLA in place, without any real examination of what it contains, and how this might need to be changed to suit your organisation's requirements.
- Hand the negotiations of the SLA to a particular

business unit, where that business unit (e.g. the IT department) does not fully consult with, or involve, other relevant business units within the organisation.

The approaches outlined above are likely to lead to problems or disputes in the provision of the services later on. This is because they move away from the general principle of making the SLA simple and workable.

A better approach is for staff and business units at your organisation who are responsible for operations, and who understand the services which are required, to work alongside lawyers (and other parties negotiating the SLA for your organisation) at an early stage, so that the SLA that is created caters for your organisation's needs.

Using specialist outsourcing lawyers (working together with relevant staff, business units and advisers at your organisation) to develop and draft your SLA can save your organisation time and money. This is because:

- Tried and tested templates can be used to begin with, and they can then tailor your SLA to your requirements.
- They can ask your organisation the right questions, and having found out the answers to these questions, can then incorporate the relevant details into the SLA.
- Their experience and industry knowledge in drafting these SLAs can be used to finalise the SLA in a short space of time.
- They will be able to advise upon areas regarding where you should, or should not, press for

provisions to be added to the SLA, based upon their industry knowledge and what the 'norm' is.

- They can draft the SLA in a way which can avoid problems or disputes in the future.

Key to all of this is your organisation and the supplier clearly defining and assigning roles to their respective staff, when those staff negotiate the SLA.

SLA documents and reality

One reason that SLAs go wrong, is that the SLA that has been negotiated, does not reflect what is happening in practice.

If the SLA does not reflect what is happening in practice, then the parties might no longer refer to, or use, the SLA, and may simply work in an *ad hoc* fashion. If this happens, then there is nothing for the parties to refer to regarding how current services should be provided, and the standards that they should achieve. To try to avoid this problem, it is important for an organisation to:

- Involve all relevant staff and business units (or representatives of these staff or business units) that will be affected by the services provided under the SLA. This will ensure that the SLA meets their needs, and any obvious errors, problems or omissions can be spotted early by such staff and business units (or their representatives), whilst the SLA is being negotiated and formulated.
- Ensure that the staff that are negotiating the SLA for the organisation, fully understand the organisation's requirements and the requirements

of the organisation's different business units. Again, if the negotiation of the SLA is left to external lawyers who have little contact or appreciation of how the services are to be provided, and how the SLA will affect the organisation and its business units in practice, then this can lead to problems later on.

Also, when talking about the drafting of the SLA, your organisation and lawyers must keep in mind that this is an ongoing relationship where the building up of trust between your organisation and the supplier is key. Because of this, your organisation should steer away from the temptation to include provisions in the SLA which are clearly not going to be acceptable to the supplier. Any attempt by your organisation to 'get one over' on the supplier, by including such obviously unacceptable provisions, could lead to problems and disputes at the start of the relationship, or later on (and at the very least, breach the trust between your organisation and the supplier).

Hence, if you do see provisions in an SLA which, although of major benefit to your organisation, you know are clearly unacceptable to the supplier (but which might have been suggested by your lawyers or other third parties advising your organisation), then it is advisable that you question whether such clauses are absolutely necessary and, if so, your organisation should be up front with the supplier and point these clauses out. If your organisation decides to retain such provisions in the SLA, in the hope that they may be useful later on, you should appreciate that this can cause problems or disputes in the future.

The unused SLA

An SLA can go wrong if it is simply not used by the parties. This could be for various reasons, such as if it is full of legalese, complicated formulas and confusing themes, or if the project personnel do not understand it, so that the SLA is simply disregarded.

The dangers with an SLA being disregarded are that:

- It can then be replaced by an unofficial 'understanding' between project managers of your organisation and the supplier, as to what is to happen regarding service provision. Problems then arise when this 'understanding' breaks down, for example, if project managers cannot subsequently agree on the standard of service provision, or if project managers leave your organisation so that there is no clarity as to what this unofficial 'understanding' between project managers consists of.
- If the SLA has been disregarded and not been used for a long time, there is a legal question as to whether or not it can still apply, whether the SLA has been replaced by the conduct of the parties (whatever that conduct may be), or whether no specific service standard needs to be adhered to.

Summary

SLAs can go wrong for a number of reasons. As mentioned above, these reasons can include:

- Your service requirements not being defined properly.

- Too many service levels and service level targets which can become difficult to manage and monitor.
- SLAs not reflecting reality.
- The SLA being prepared, or negotiated, by the wrong people at your organisation.
- SLAs being so complicated that they are not used by project personnel.

The next chapter explains how you can build the foundation for your SLA, including fully understanding, and spelling out, what your own needs are, and what your requirements are of the supplier.

CHAPTER 3: BUILDING THE FOUNDATION FOR THE SLA

It is often the case that SLAs are only thought about by organisations either once they start to talk to potential suppliers, or, alternatively, towards the end of negotiating the framework agreement, when time is short and a deal needs to be signed imminently. However, rushing the preparation and thought behind the SLA can lead to problems later on.

In this chapter, we look at what elements you should be considering, well before even engaging with potential suppliers.

Your organisation should consider what it would require regarding services, and the standard of services to be provided. Going through such a process will help to crystallise your organisation's thoughts about what it needs, and will enable it to sort through various supplier proposals, in order to find the proposal which most closely matches its needs.

However, going through this thought process and documenting it, will take your organisation some time. As well as taking into account the issues in Chapters 1 and 2, some other specific issues which an organisation should consider are addressed in this chapter.

Codify existing services and standards

An organisation needs to understand what services it is currently obtaining, the standards of those services, and the cost of those services.

Some of the initial questions that an organisation is likely to be asked by a potential supplier, are:

- What services and service standards does your organisation already have in place?
- How often do services meet requirements?
- How much do these services currently cost your organisation?

Of the services that your organisation currently has in place, which ones are the most useful and the least useful, which specific services are the most problematic, which services are used regularly, and which ones are rarely used or never used?

Without this information, your organisation (and any potential supplier) cannot really compare the services and standards which it currently receives (and the cost of these services) with any potential services (and associated costs) that a potential supplier is proposing. Also, if a potential supplier is proposing to provide equivalent services to what your organisation already uses, but at a much lower cost (say, 50% of what your organisation is currently paying), then this might also make your organisation check and enquire as to how such savings are going to be made by the supplier (in order to ensure that the supplier is not over promising, in respect of what it can actually deliver).

Hence, work will need to be done to find out about this and also to codify this information into something which the people making the decisions regarding any potential supplier proposals, can easily understand. It may well be that the reason that potential suppliers are being considered in the first place, is that there is some dissatisfaction with the existing services and/or their cost, but it could well be that this has been misunderstood, or that your organisation is actually paying a lot less for services than it actually realises.

Without the information above, it becomes incredibly difficult for an organisation to make rational decisions about whether or not the proposals submitted by potential suppliers represent value for money, and so codifying what is currently in place is a good first step.

Having this information to hand also helps your organisation in negotiations regarding the SLA. This is because an organisation can, if it wishes, explain to the potential suppliers in any negotiations, that it already receives certain services for a certain price. Hence, it would not make commercial sense for your organisation to engage suppliers if they are going to provide less services or standards for the same price, or if they intend to provide equivalent services or standards but at a higher price!

However, many organisations do not have this information to hand, and may not have gone through the process of assessing the IT that they use, and how much this costs in total. Hence, codifying such information might be a detailed and time consuming exercise, but one which is well worthwhile (even if this just helps an organisation understand its own IT systems and costs better). I have seen organisations go through the exercise of codifying their own IT systems and cost, comparing this with the proposals of external suppliers, and then subsequently choosing to stay with what they already have (rather than choosing an external supplier) because what they already have represents a good service for the price that is being paid.

Without information about an organisation's IT systems, an organisation can flounder in talks with suppliers when asked specific questions as to what services, what standards, and what cost the current services are being provided at. In the absence of information provided by your organisation, the supplier may well assume that:

- Your organisation is very dissatisfied with the current services and their cost (as otherwise it would probably not even be talking to the supplier), such that the supplier has free range to charge as much as it can.
- Your organisation does not know what it is receiving and so the supplier may make assumptions as to what it thinks is happening and present these to your organisation. The gist of this might generally be that very little service, or a poor service, is being provided at a very high cost. When calculating the cost of provision of service, the supplier might take numerous items into account to emphasise the point that your organisation's existing service is very costly (this could include not only staff costs and benefits, but also factoring in premises, IT equipment, etc. that relate to service provision), in order to make the supplier's services (and associated costs) look attractive.
- The supplier may then base its proposal on its own assumptions about what the current service

levels and costs are (and taking everything into account regarding what it thinks your organisation's current costs are for IT) and then price its proposal accordingly. The typical gist being, that it will provide much more service, but for the same cost (or a slightly reduced cost).

The message is clear – an organisation needs to be clear about what service it is receiving and the cost of this, in order to accurately assess whether or not services offered by a supplier represent real value for money.

What services do you want (and need)?

The definition of services must all be addressed in the SLA, i.e.:

- What is to be included in the services.
- What is not to be included in the services.
- What additional services can be provided and how much they will cost.
- What additional services cannot or will not be provided.

One key dispute area between parties can be what is included, and what is not included in the services (and the associated costs).

Because of this, your organisation should also fully understand what it needs (i.e. what is the basic service required?), as well as what it wants (i.e. the ideal service). As part of this exercise, your organisation needs to be clear about the services which it does not want (and hence services which it does not want to pay for).

The EDS/Fujitsu Case Study[3] below shows that problems can arise if the SLA (or related documentation) does not spell out exactly what services are to be provided, at what cost (and to identify any services that are not included in the price).

For more than 10 years, EDS had been providing IT services to various government departments, including the Department for Work and Pensions (DWP).

The services included the development, maintenance and operation of software applications used by the DWP, on mainframe computers. Fujitsu had supplied the mainframe computers and software throughout. The mainframe computers that Fujitsu either leased or sold to EDS, operated on Fujitsu's proprietary operating systems, known as 'Virtual Machine Environment' (VME).

Fujitsu licensed EDS to use the VME system and associated software, and Fujitsu also provided maintenance for the mainframes. The parties used a measure of computing capacity of the relevant mainframes known as MIPS (millions of instructions per second), in order to ascertain the relevant charges under the agreement.

The action was brought following a dispute between the parties as to whether a particular cost had been incorporated into the various agreements.

The dispute before the court concerned the charging for

---

3 Fujitsu Services Limited v Electronic Data Systems Limited (EDS) [2008] EWHC 211.

software licensing and system service for three mainframe computers used by EDS for business continuity purposes (i.e. disaster recovery back-up). Fujitsu submitted that it was owed the additional payment by virtue of:

- The applicable payment obligations.
- An implied term; and/or
- *Quantum meruit* (i.e. being paid a reasonable amount of money for work done).

The court:

- Rejected Fujitsu's claim that EDS payment obligations were as submitted by Fujitsu.
- Ruled that Fujitsu was not entitled to receive the additional payments via an implied term or *quantum meruit*.

The court's view was that Fujitsu had had ample opportunity to rectify the alleged 'oversight' on several occasions, but this had not been picked up by Fujitsu's management team who had reviewed the documentation (pursuant to yearly audits of the equipment being supplied to EDS).

In summary, EDS had used equipment for which it had not been charged, but Fujitsu should have picked this up earlier, and so could not recover back payments. However, if the goods and services to be provided had been specifically laid out in an SLA (or similar agreement), and costed, then this dispute may never have arisen.

Same service cheaper?

In terms of strategy, an organisation needs to be clear about what exactly it is trying to achieve. If cost savings are the desired result, then spending more on new services does not make commercial sense (unless the savings delivered by such extra spending are justifiable).

Alternatively, if the strategy of an organisation is to obtain an acceptable service, or a better service, then it may have to accept that this might well involve additional cost (even if the supplier can make efficiency savings). In this case, a key question will be how much extra is your organisation prepared to pay for an improved service?

The simple point is that if your organisation wants a much better service, then it might have to pay more for this service, and your organisation needs to be sure that it can afford the costs involved before embarking on an IT project, rather than finding out later on that it cannot (or could never) afford the services that the supplier is proposing.

A common assumption when defining the services required, is that your organisation wants the same service, performed to the same standard, but at less cost. However, this assumption does not always hold true. For example, one of the reasons that your organisation was alerted to the issue of services may well be that service was poor. It might only be after that point that an internal review started, which uncovered that you were paying more for the services than you thought.

The key here is to understand that:

- Organisations often want a better service than they had before, otherwise they would not be in talks with potential suppliers. Better service can incorporate many aspects, including more technically advanced goods (e.g. higher specification software and hardware), better response times, more skilled and experienced personnel doing the work, leading to better and quicker solutions, more reports from the supplier as to what is happening and how the supplier is performing, provision of industry knowledge and ideas for cost-savings, together with more review meetings to monitor and manage the services. All of this often comes at a higher price.
- Organisations are often opened up to a menu of other tempting, different, or improved services, which they would otherwise be unaware of. The supplier may also be keen to sell in more services to your organisation. However, although this could have potential benefits for your organisation, this will often cost more.

So, the question about what service you want is not as simple as it first looks because this may come at a price which is more than you are willing to pay. It is also important to factor in the cost your organisation will incur in actually negotiating and preparing the SLA (i.e. deal costs). For example, your organisation may have to dedicate staff and resources to negotiating the SLA with a supplier, and may also incur external legal costs for legal advice that it might need regarding the negotiation and drafting of the SLA.

The ideal situation is to obtain a much better service at much less cost. However, in many cases, your organisation might have to accept that this ideal position might not, or cannot, be achieved in practice (or that this ideal position can only be achieved towards the end of the contract term, which might be many years away).

What are your organisation's responsibilities?

Some people may think that the SLA is all 'one way', in that the supplier provides all of the services, and all that your organisation needs to do is to pay for these services.

However, if your organisation simply abandons its responsibilities regarding its own IT, and leaves this all to the supplier, then this can cause major problems.

For example:

- Your organisation will not fully understand how your IT is configured.
- Your organisation will not fully understand how your IT is operated.
- Without an understanding of your IT, your organisation will not be able to fully control it.
- Your organisation will be 100% reliant on, or led by, the advice and recommendations of your supplier (without being able to double check, or challenge this advice and recommendations, since you may not fully understand what your IT systems consist of, how your IT systems have developed over time, or how they have been modified over time).

Because of all of this, it is important that your organisation does not hand over all decisions, management and control of your IT systems to a supplier, such that your organisation loses touch with, and knowledge about, its own IT systems. A better approach is to have employees or consultants engaged directly by, and working for and on behalf of, your organisation (e.g. IT directors, IT consultants or IT project managers, etc.) so that they can oversee or direct what the supplier is doing. These staff can then report back to your organisation, with an independent opinion on what exactly is happening and why, so that your organisation can make fully informed decisions.

Template SLAs

A template of an SLA can be a useful start and can save time and money. A template can help an organisation to order and assemble its thoughts, and also helps to focus on areas where it needs further information. Your organisation can then build upon this SLA depending upon its exact requirements.

In addition, your organisation could ask potential suppliers to provide SLAs in their proposals. This will often provide your organisation with additional ideas about requirements that it should add to the SLA. Hence, the final SLA can often be a document which merges elements of your organisation's SLA, with elements of the supplier's SLA.

However, when working on an SLA, it is important to have it produced and/or reviewed by specialist outsourcing lawyers, to ensure that it will work from a legal point of view. This will include ensuring that it ties in properly with the framework agreement and any other documents relating to the deal as a whole.

There are many templates or precedents available to help you create your SLA with your supplier. These can be obtained from reference books, the Internet, or from other organisations which you have dealt with.

Although templates are sometimes a good start to creating your SLA, I would recommend that you use your outsourcing lawyers in preparing and working on an SLA for your organisation. This is because many of the templates I have seen that are available on the Internet, or are produced by private companies and sold in pdf format on the Internet:

- Do not cover the deal envisaged by your organisation (which can mean that your organisation can end up using the wrong type of document for a deal, so that it means that the deal has to bend to the document, rather than the document reflecting the deal). This can, in turn, cause a variety of problems and lead to the parties arguing over deal structure.
- Have some clauses which simply do not work, either in law or in practice. Hence, this can lead to SLAs which are destined to not only cause practical problems and arguments, but also to create major legal problems if such clauses are ever scrutinised by the courts.
- Do not fit in with any other transactions that the SLA forms part of. For example, a normal IT outsourcing deal may have various legal aspects

covering IT, premises, employment, pensions, tax, competition law, corporate law and intellectual property, so that a standard SLA template may not be geared to take account of these legal issues.

Hence, in summary, SLA templates can be useful food for thought, but an organisation should really obtain its SLA from its specialist outsourcing lawyers (or at least involve its lawyers in the process of creating or developing an SLA) because otherwise this could simply store up problems for the future (which could be time consuming and costly to resolve).

Setting service levels and targets

A fundamental point to SLAs is that, if you set various service levels and service level targets you should, if those targets are met, have a good service which you are happy with. However, a key to this, is being able to articulate and explain the desired output or outcomes from the services and then accurately reflecting this by:

- Choosing the right service levels and the right service level targets.
- Choosing the right number of service levels and service level targets.
- Prioritising service levels and service level targets.
- Setting the value of any service level credits at a level that properly compensates you.

The danger is that, if you do not do this properly, then:

- The supplier could hit or exceed all of the service levels and targets you have set, but you are still receiving a poor service, or not achieving the desired output or outcome.

- There are too many service levels and targets, so that it is difficult to monitor and manage (and the focus on targets being met can replace the desired outcomes or outputs and what the SLA is trying to achieve overall).
- Certain service levels and service level targets are always achieved but these are not a priority for you, whereas more important targets are not achieved (i.e. even though certain service levels and targets are achieved, this does not produce the desired outcomes and outputs).
- Any compensation your organisation obtains is nominal compared to the damage done by targets not being met.

A common problem here is that in negotiations, a supplier may suggest that a service level target is set at, say, 98%. However, your organisation may counter and insist that the service level target is set at, say, 99%. This may well be necessary, but in negotiations, be aware of the temptation to automatically insist on increased service level targets for each service level, simply because it appears as though this will automatically achieve a better service for your organisation. For example, in negotiations, parties (or their lawyers) who might argue for a service level target of 99% rather than 98%:

- May not fully understand the services to which this percentage applies (e.g. if this is negotiated by lawyers or sales people who do not deal with the day-to-day technical aspects of the service provision and how it might benefit your organisation).

- May not be fully aware of what exactly the impact of this extra one per cent is (i.e. does it make any significant difference to your organisation?).
- May focus on battling for this extra one per cent to achieve a moral victory in negotiations over the supplier (but may well just simply be unwittingly reallocating the supplier's time, effort and resources to achieving results in a specific area, which is far in excess of what your organisation really needs).

For example, you may insist that a service level report is provided by the supplier to your organisation within seven days of the end of each month. The target for doing this might be that this must happen at least 98% of the time. However, some organisations may spend a long time negotiating with the supplier to insist that this must happen 99% of the time. In this case, an organisation has to be aware that it might well get the report each month in any event and so it will need to assess whether or not spending time, effort and money negotiating this point is actually worth the benefit of any increase in a service level target percentage.

Condensing service levels

You may want a supplier to:

- Respond to your problems within 10 minutes of notification.
- Start working on any reported problems immediately.
- Keep you informed every 10 minutes as to what

the status of the problem resolution is.
- Use various techniques and methods to solve the problem.
- Dedicate as many people as it takes to sort out the problem as soon as possible.
- Provide a report on the problem, who dealt with it, and the time taken to resolve it, for each problem dealt with.

However, it could be possible to cover this desired output or outcome by converting all of this information into one service level, to say that problems need to be fixed within one hour of them being reported, and a proforma report needs to be completed regarding each problem.

Accurately converting your desired outputs or outcomes into a few clear service levels and service level targets can help to achieve a better service because:

- It provides an objective measure as to whether a target has been achieved or not.
- It provides clarity for the supplier so that a supplier is not distracted by numerous subjective requirements (some of which may only be of passing interest to your organisation).
- It allows the supplier to focus its budgeted time and resources on service levels which really matter to your organisation, rather than spreading its budgeted time and resources thinly in an attempt to meet dozens of service level targets.

There should be some prioritisation of problems, so that major catastrophic problems (e.g. the whole IT network shutting down) have to be resolved quickly and are differentiated from relatively minor problems which the supplier can take longer to fix (e.g. a computer screen that might flicker occasionally).

It is also important to understand and document what levels of service would seem to be very good, acceptable, poor, and unacceptable, and then try to link these into percentages relating to how often the service level target has been met. For example, if the service level target is met 99%+ of the time, then this could be classed as 'good'. 95% to 99% could be classed as 'acceptable', 90% to 95% could be classed as 'poor' and below 90% could be classed as 'unacceptable'.

If 99% was the target level, then it could mean that each percentage point (or part thereof) below that level would attract compensation of £x payable to your organisation (via a service credit) down to 95%. However, it could be that, if service drops to between 90% to 95%, extra compensation is payable and additional remedial action may need to be taken by the supplier. If the service drops further to below 90%, then, as well as even more compensation and additional remedial action, this could give your organisation the right to terminate the whole deal.

Who calculates the service credits?

The responsibility for monitoring the service levels and associated service credits usually rests with the supplier (but the SLA should make this supplier since it will have records of how the services have been provided and to what standard (for example, when faults were reported and how quickly they were resolved).

Otherwise, if this were left to your organisation, then this would (in part) defeat the point of it having a supplier provide services to it, since your organisation wants to be free to concentrate on its core business. As part of this process, the supplier would be obliged to keep accurate, up-to-date, and complete records of the services it provides to your organisation (including how it has achieved, regarding meeting service level targets). These records should be open to inspection by your organisation.

The SLA report

It is important to specify at the outset the format, detail and frequency of service level reporting and what your organisation expects. This is because suppliers may have a standard way of reporting this (e.g. by simply providing numbers and tables and spreadsheets), yet this may not be everything that your organisation requires.

For example, your organisation may wish the supplier to not only provide raw data to show how standards/targets have been addressed, but also to provide a comprehensive narrative upon:

1. The general service over the time period that the report covers, and the total service credits due (if any).
2. How this report compares to the previous report, for example, any major problems from the previous report that have now been resolved during this reporting period.
3. Any new or major issues that have occurred over this reporting period (and why they occurred, what was done to resolve them, and recommendations as to how these can be avoided in future).
4. Any ongoing issues that continue to occur and

recommendations on how to mitigate, or eliminate, these issues, in order to provide a better service.

It is important in an SLA to obtain information in a way which is easily understandable and digestible. What you do not want to have to do is to pore through 'raw data' to try to find out what is actually happening.

You could specify in your SLA that monthly reports have a number of sections, which are divided as follows:

- A one-page 'dashboard' (providing graphs, charts and pie charts of what is happening, so you can easily see at a glance what the profile of the service standard actually is).
- A report with more detailed analysis of the service standards (perhaps incorporating (1) – (4) above).
- A schedule of any specific raw data which is used in support of (1) and (2) above.

A one-page monthly dashboard could include the elements in the following graph.

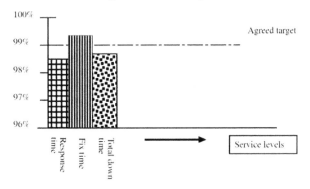

Figure 1: An example of a one-page monthly dashboard

You could request a number of charts for your chosen variables, so that you get the picture at a glance. You could also request pie charts, which divide out various issues, to provide a graphical depiction of your service profile.

In the pie chart on the following page, you can see, at a glance, the problems that the supplier and your organisation are facing.

▨ Hardware issues

▬ End-user calls re PCs

▤ Internet connection problems

▨ Software issues

▨ Network issues

Figure 2: Division of problems arising in them month

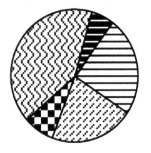

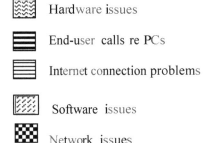

**Figure 3: Time spent by supplier resolving
different issues**

From this dashboard layout, you can see that it appears
that most of the problems are arising from hardware
issues, and that the supplier is spending most of its time
dealing with these hardware issues. Questions that might
arise from these charts, include:

• Why are there so many problems with the
hardware?

- Is the resolving of issues regarding hardware an organisational priority? If not, then what can be done to ensure problems regarding hardware can be addressed, so that the supplier is 'freed up' to spend its time more usefully on more important organisational priorities?
- Should your organisation look at changing, modifying or upgrading its hardware, in order to avoid so many problems, or should it perhaps obtain different hardware from different suppliers?

SLA meetings

The IT outsourcing contract and/or SLA will often cater for meetings to occur to review services at regular intervals, such as monthly or quarterly.

These are good times to review the service and also discuss problems that have occurred and what is needed. Often these meetings will be minuted, and so it is important for the parties to include any major issues or problems in those minutes (even if this does not assign blame to whose fault this was).

This is because, if the service deteriorates over time, then these regular minutes will provide a useful summary of how services have been provided. The danger is that, if major problems or concerns have not been minuted at meetings, and your organisation later claims that the services were not adequate, then this claim can, on the face of it, be countered by a supplier. The supplier may state that it was unaware of your organisation's issues or problems (or only became recently aware of these), because this had not been raised or minuted at any of the meetings between your organisation and the supplier.

SLA tiers

Often a supplier will propose a service which it can provide, and then an organisation may simply be happy to accept that service, with the associated service levels and targets. However, and as mentioned above, many organisations will need to modify services and service standards in certain circumstances (e.g. if your organisation and its business is heavily regulated, etc.).

Other examples of tiers of service include:

- **A VIP service** – here the supplier may be obliged to prioritise staff requests, so that if queries/issues are logged by the CEO or senior management team of your organisation, then these will be dealt with first, on an urgent basis (rather than simply joining the queue of requests from other people in your organisation).
- **Timing** – although you may want the service provided to be satisfactory at all times, there may be particular times in the year when the service being provided to standard is absolutely critical, compared to other times in the year. For example, the months immediately preceding your organisation's financial year end, or designated reporting dates.
- **Key clients** – if the service is affected, then your organisation may have key clients which this affects. Your organisation may (if it is possible) designate that if the poor service affects all clients, then there is a list of key clients to which normal service will be restored as soon as possible (if

prioritisation is possible, regarding the fault in question).

- **End-user consideration** – in negotiating an SLA, your organisation may get drawn into simply focusing upon the services offered by the supplier and trying to negotiate a better service (via perhaps increased service level targets). However, it is important to remember that if the services are to be provided to your end-users (both staff internally and external third parties), then their needs and requirements need to be considered and added to any services, service levels and service level targets. It may be that your organisation already has feedback from end-users regarding services (or it might ask end-users what they would like to see regarding services). All of this information can be fed into the SLA, in order to ensure that it captures services which the end-users at your organisation want.

- **Changes** – it is not unusual for your organisation to request changes to the services required, particularly if the services are provided over a long period of time. However, it is important to put procedures into the SLA in order to cater for an orderly management of changes (*See Chapter 2*).

- **Priorities** – it is useful to pre-define the class of problem or issue that might occur (in a generic way), together with the response time and remedies associated with such a class of problem. For example, a critical problem may be if your organisation's whole IT system is inoperable for more than 30 minutes, and the response time might be that it must be fixed within two hours. The remedies may include compensation and also invoking an action plan (involving update meetings and a certain number of staff being devoted to fixing the problem). However, there may be another class of problem which is where this causes minor inconvenience (such as a screen that flickers occasionally) and the response time for this might be two days, and the remedies might not include compensation or invoking any type of action plan.

Summary

As can be seen from the above, there are a number of issues for your organisation to consider when building the foundation of an SLA, and even before approaching potential suppliers and drafting the SLA. It is important to consider these issues beforehand, so that you have a good understanding of your needs, budget, strategy and vision regarding your IT systems, before you talk to potential suppliers.

The next chapter talks about things to consider when drafting the SLA itself.

CHAPTER 4: DRAFTING THE SLA AND KEY CLAUSES

This chapter covers the issues to consider when drafting an SLA.

Drafting the SLA will typically involve:

- Obtaining a template for an SLA from your organisation's specialist outsourcing lawyers.
- Working on that SLA to tailor it to your requirements by adding in the information from the previous chapters.
- Adding bespoke provisions which suit the particular needs of your organisation.
- Tying in the SLA to the framework agreement, YET ensuring the SLA can operate as a stand-alone working document (rather than IT managers having always to refer back to the IT outsourcing agreement which may well be voluminous).
- Understanding that the framework agreement often has extensive provisions, many of which will fall away and expire soon after the IT deal is entered into, because of the fact that the activities specified will be performed on the date of signature of the deal, or shortly afterwards. Such activities can include items such as payments up front, transfer of employee clauses, transfer of premises, etc. However, the SLA will be a living and evolving document throughout the term of the framework agreement.

There are certain provisions in SLAs which either

should, or should not, appear. This chapter describes some of the clauses which you should normally include in an SLA, and some of the clauses which you would *not* normally include.

Key clauses normally included in SLAs

One service credit

Identifying where your organisation can, and cannot, claim more than one service credit (especially if this is essentially for the same breach). For example, if an engineer is obliged to turn up to fix problems on site within four hours and only does so after six hours, then there may be a service credit for this. However, because of the delay there is a knock on effect of this to the uptime of the service, thereby attracting another credit. Because the uptime was not as it should be, other credits might come into play.

However, the supplier may say that only the credit for the engineer turning up late should apply, rather than all of the subsequent credits which were as a result of essentially the same breach (i.e. the engineer turning up late).

Service credit cap

If the supplier does agree to pay service credits for missing pre-agreed targets, then there will be a cap on how much the supplier is prepared to refund. Otherwise, there could come a point where, in fact, the amount of refunds significantly eats into the value of the contract as a whole for the supplier, thereby making it economically unviable.

Typically, the cap is set at somewhere between five to 15 per cent of the contract price, although this can vary from contract to contract, depending upon the bargaining positions of the parties, the value of the contract, and how much profit the supplier is making on the contract.

From the supplier's point of view, this also ensures that your organisation does not try to essentially get the vast majority of its money back, via claiming service credits, if it is trying to save as much money as possible on the contract, or trying to press for service credit in order to obtain an unofficial discount.

Service credit value

The value of a service credit will be negotiated and pre-agreed between the parties, as to what amount of compensation is due if particular targets are not met. As explained below (*see the Penalties section, p78*), although these service credit amounts should not amount to penalties (i.e. they should not be too high), if an amount is pre-agreed then it is difficult for the supplier to say at a later date that the pre-agreed amount is too high (such that it is a penalty clause that is void).

If you agree service credits with the supplier, which are proportionate to the loss your organisation is likely to suffer (and are not so much more above any loss that your organisation is likely to suffer), then such service credits are likely to be seen as fair and reasonable and legally enforceable (and are not likely to be seen as penalty clauses). The problem with a clause being deemed to be a penalty clause (i.e. where the compensation provided for as a service credit is much more than the loss that is likely to be suffered by your organisation), is that a court could deem that clause to be void and unenforceable. This would mean that if your organisation tried to enforce that clause against the supplier to obtain the relevant credits, then the supplier may argue that it does not have to pay the service credits which are stated in that clause because they are far higher than the loss that you have actually suffered.

Service level and service credit refresh

After a certain period of time, the supplier may well have got used to achieving service level targets on a regular basis without much effort, by implementing certain systems and processes. However, in this case, you may still want a better service, and so you may want the option to replace service level targets which are regularly hit with other service levels and targets which you believe are not being provided as part of the service.

For example, you may have a target that an automated report has to be provided within two days of the end of each month by the supplier. You might find that this always happens, and so is always at 100%.

So, you may then wish to replace this service level with another service level which you believe would improve the service. For example, with major problems you may wish to be called with ongoing updates and a full explanation of what happened, within a week of the problem occurring, and you may wish to add this as a service level in place of the report provision being measured (although on the understanding that the report will still need to be produced each month).

The point here is that by replacing and reworking service levels and service level credits, your organisation can mould the services which it requires to its ongoing needs (rather than being stuck with the service levels and service level credits which it specified at the start of the deal, which were set to meet its requirements at that point but where these requirements have now changed).

It is important to note that, if you want service level and service credit refresh options, then you will need to have provisions in the SLA which cater for this. These provisions will also need to explain the circumstances and terms upon which you can invoke such refreshes.

Service credit bonuses

If a service level target is set at 99%, should the supplier obtain a bonus if it exceeds this level of service? Some people believe that no such bonus should apply, since the supplier should provide 100% all of the time. The argument is that a target of 99% is giving the supplier some grace in the first place, by allowing it to be one per cent below what it should be doing (and without the supplier having to pay any compensation).

Others believe that it may be worth incentivising the supplier to achieve 100% by paying extra (via a bonus) for that extra one per cent (or part of that), such that the supplier is focused and motivated to achieve a premium service.

There are some other ways to provide bonus like

schemes, such as:

- Allowing the supplier to earn or 'win back' bonuses against credits which are paid, or payable by the supplier, in any particular period. For example, if the supplier owes your organisation £5,000 in credits for a quarter, if it has built up bonuses in the previous quarter which amount to £3,000, then you may allow the supplier to only pay you £2,000 in credits.
- Paying discretionary bonuses directly to the staff of the supplier that is providing the services to your organisation over a particular period of time (rather than any bonus money going to the supplier itself).
- Thinking about ongoing bonus structures. This is because in long-term contracts the initial excitement and motivation of the supplier following a contract win can wane over time, leading to a steady and gradual decline in the standard of service provided.

In summary, some people believe that the deterrent to the supplier of paying service credits should suffice in an SLA. However, it is always worth considering if you can incentivise the supplier to achieve certain goals which lead to the provision of a good service and ongoing motivation for a supplier over a long period of time.

Trends

It is common for SLAs to measure services over either a month or a quarter, with credits being payable if services are not met over that period.

The reason for this is that, if services are measured over short periods (e.g. a day), with service credits being payable if services do not meet the pre- agreed levels for that day, then:

- This leaves little time for the supplier to make good any default to avoid paying a credit.
- The measuring, administration and reporting of the service levels and credits becomes cumbersome and time-consuming.
- This does not give a true picture of the service being provided, since it is measured over such a short period (and penalises the supplier for 'one-off' blips in services).

If a supplier thinks it is going to have to pay a credit anyway over a short period (e.g. a day), then if a problem does occur and a credit is payable anyway, then the supplier's motivation to remedy the problem may be diminished.

Therefore, it is recommended that service levels, targets and credits are measured and managed over longer periods (e.g. a quarter), so that a true picture of the service can be established and suppliers are not penalised for 'blips' in the service, where there may be a problem for a particular day but this is not typical of the service overall. However, if there are significant specific breaches of service levels that your organisation is particularly concerned about, then it may try to cater for those by having particular service credits payable for these particular breaches (regardless of what the trend might be regarding these significant specific breaches).

Flexibility

It is inevitable in a long-term relationship that your requirements will change over time. This might be because your organisation may merge or restructure, move location, require more or less service, or require different services altogether.

Some of these events can be foreseen and planned for (at least in part) at the time that the SLA is entered into. For example:

- Do you have the right to reduce services if required and get a proportionate reduction in the amount of money you pay for this service (although the supplier will want you to commit to paying for at least a minimum amount of service over any particular period, whether you need it or not)?
- Do you have the right to increase the services required and is this at a price which is pro- rated upwards for the extra service? A complication can occur here since in some service contracts the supplier will incur a significant cost increase or step change if extra services are required.

For example, your organisation may incur a 'step change cost' if it is using the supplier to provide data processing and storage services using the supplier's existing servers, but wants additional data processing capacity and ability. This additional data processing capacity and ability may only be able to be provided if the supplier purchases new equipment (i.e. new servers), or moves to new premises, in order to process and store your additional data. This is referred to as a 'step change cost' because rather than the supplier being able to use its existing equipment (and just charge your organisation slightly more for the additional data processing), the supplier has had to go out and invest more money in more equipment and/or premises. The supplier will want to pass on the significant cost of this to your organisation (and this cost will be much more than simply paying for additional data to be processed on a pro-rated basis, based upon the amount of data processed prior to the request for additional data processing).

For example, your organisation may have paid, say, £1,000, to have data processed for it encapsulating 15,000 client matters on the database. Your organisation may now want to ask the supplier to process an extra 15,000 client matters on the database (making 30,000 client matters in all) and your organisation might expect that this will simply cost £2,000 (since it is double the number of client matters originally processed). However, because the supplier might have to purchase additional equipment and/or take on new premises to process these extra client matters, it may be that the additional 15,000 client matters actually costs £4,000 to process (making a total of £5,000 for 30,000 client matters). This example simply demonstrates that your organisation cannot simply assume that it can scale up its requirements of the IT supplier and simply expect that prices will remain in line with the prices that have been charged in the past.

If the amount of services which you require is unlikely to stay static over the term of the contract, then it is worthwhile investigating the costs of increasing or decreasing the services that you may want, and seeing if the consequences of this (including the changes in cost) are acceptable to you.

If it is likely that you might need additional or completely different services during the contract term, then how much are such services likely to cost? It can be difficult to assess this at the time of entering into an SLA but you may be able to:

- Fix the hourly rates of the supplier for the term of the contract.
- Fix the rates for certain goods and services for the term of the contract. If you need more of these goods and services, you may want to pay the same price that you did for the original orders.
- Agree some fixed mark up or profit margin by the supplier on completely different goods and/or services you might order during the term, so that you are not faced with incredibly high fees for extra goods and/or services, but are locked into ordering these from the incumbent supplier.
- Agree some arrangement whereby if you need extra goods and/or services, the price of these will be benchmarked against what you can get in the market from other suppliers at the time, so that you do not end up paying much more.

Some of these provisions may well be resisted by a supplier for various reasons; it may be that it has its own pricing models for each deal and cannot simply lock itself in to certain prices on day one of the SLA.

However, the best time to ask the questions above is when you have a number of possible suppliers and at the time when your bargaining position might be the strongest (which is before making the final decision about your preferred supplier).

Communication

Building a good working relationship with your supplier is sometimes underestimated, in that your organisation may simply view the supplier as a third party contractor doing work for you for money (and providing limited refunds where defaults occur, via service credits).

However, it is essential that communication is maintained and formalised either in the framework agreement or the SLA. For example, the SLA can provide that:

- There are regular meetings (e.g. perhaps once a month initially and then, once you are happy with the service, these could move to once per quarter).
- Certain people must attend these meetings (this may include the project manager, plus the supplier's CIO or IT director, or a member of the supplier's senior management team). Having a member of the supplier's senior management team at such a meeting can make that person aware of your satisfaction (or otherwise) with the service provided. It is worth noting that negative comments made by you to the project manager at the IT supplier on a day-to-day basis, may not reach the senior management team at the supplier. Hence, meeting the senior management team at the supplier gives you an opportunity to put your points directly to them.
- Minutes of each meeting are taken and approved by the parties (together with action points allocated to each party and individuals). This

written record will also come in useful if there are any disputes which subsequently arise regarding the services.

- The supplier can inform you of anything which it believes your organisation is not doing properly, or which is preventing the supplier from providing the best service possible. This is an early warning system, particularly if the supplier is laying the ground for blaming your organisation for the way or manner in which you are using the services, in order for them to avoid having to pay credits, or avoid claims or legal action later on. Therefore, it is always useful for you to know if the supplier has any issues and, if it does, then to document and address them as soon as possible.

Worked examples

It is often the case that due to the wide-ranging and diverse services that might be provided by the supplier, the service levels, service level targets, and service level credits can become complicated.

Worked examples might include formulas which have notional values inserted into them to show how these might work in practice. For example, when calculating uptime of the system the calculation might be set out as:

Uptime = Hours that the system is available during 9am – 5pm divided by eight.

Therefore, uptime could be five hours in a particular day, divided by eight (being the total office hours) = 62.5% uptime.

However, what about scheduled maintenance? It may be that the reason that the three hours down time occurred in the calculation above, is that the system was down for scheduled maintenance. Again, this has to be factored into this calculation. By having this explanation and using notional numbers, this helps the parties prepare formulas and calculate actual values in reality.

Including worked examples of how things are to operate in practice means that:

- Any ambiguity is clarified in the wording of any description that describes what is meant to happen in terms of service credits.
- Running notional numbers through a worked example and formulas often highlights and flushes out deficiencies or errors in the actual method of how service credits are calculated. These can then be addressed in the SLA, rather than leading to disputes later on.
- The parties understand and can see what credits are payable and owed, so that they are comfortable with this.

For example, it can often come as a surprise to your organisation (when worked examples are not used) that a service credit might be based upon the service charge for that particular item of service (rather than the whole service) per month, divided by the number of days in the month, and then perhaps divided again by various factors (i.e. if some use of the item was achieved during that day, perhaps the credit is just based upon the number of working hours that the item was not operational).

This whittling down of the credit may not be apparent unless worked examples are employed in the SLA to see what exactly this credit amounts to in monetary terms.

Clauses not normally included in SLAs

Penalties

When talking generally about service levels and targets, people often refer to penalties being applicable when targets are not met. However, in English law you are generally only allowed to claim for the loss you have suffered (and not more than that) if an obligation has not been met. You should not be able to make a profit out of your loss so, for example, if you have lost £1,000 because a target has not been met, then you should only be entitled to recover £1,000 and not recover a higher amount such as £5,000 (whereby the additional £4,000 is intended to be a penalty). The problem with referring to penalty clauses in an SLA is that this suggests that you are claiming for more than you have actually lost. Because of this, such clauses could be challenged by the supplier as constituting a penalty against it, and, therefore, could be deemed by the court to be void or unenforceable.

Hence, these 'penalties' are often referred to as 'service credits', where the service credits are a pre-agreed amount of compensation (i.e. liquidated damages) for a pre-agreed event.

A liquidated damages clause must be a genuine pre-estimate of loss, otherwise it will be viewed by the court as an invalid penalty clause. The courts will not uphold a contractual requirement to pay liquidated damages, if it is shown that the object and effect of that provision is to deter the breaching party from breaking their contract by imposing on them, if they do so, a penalty in excess of the damages otherwise recoverable (Bridge v Campbell Discount Co Ltd [1962] AC 600).

The test for distinguishing penalties from liquidated damages is set out in Dunlop Pneumatic Tyre Co Limited v New Garage and Motor Co Limited [1915] AC 79, and is broadly defined as follows:

- A clause will be construed as a penalty clause if the sum specified is 'extravagant and unconscionable' in comparison with the greatest loss that could possibly have been proved as a result of the breach.
- It is likely to be a penalty if the breach of contract consists of not paying a sum of money, and the sum stipulated as damages is greater than the sum which ought to have been paid.
- There is a presumption that if the same sum is stated to apply to different types of breach of contract, some of which are serious and others not, it is likely to be a penalty clause.
- It is not a bar to the operation of a liquidated damages clause that a precise pre-estimation is impossible.

Factors the court will take into account when making this decision:

- Equality of bargaining power. In particular (see Tullett Prebon Group Limited v Ghaleb

El-Hajjali [2008] EWHC 1924), the fact that the other party were represented by solicitors and could negotiate changes to the contract that were to its benefit.

- Estimating the loss. The preparation of some form of financial assessment will be helpful. It should not be hard to prepare a calculation of the predicted losses before entering into the contract and this can then be used as evidence.
- Discuss and agree with the other side. It would be sensible to discuss any calculations and agree, as far as possible, the amount payable under the liquidated damages clause.
- Purpose of the clause. While this may be difficult in practice, the party in whose favour the clause operates should seek to ensure that the aim of the clause is to compensate for breach, rather than to deter the other party from breaching the agreement. In practice, this will be difficult to do if the amount is not a genuine pre-estimate of loss.

Examples from case law

Volkswagen Financial Services (UK) Ltd v George Ramage [2007] CC (Cambridge)

An owner needed to carry out some form of calculation to see what loss there might be, otherwise it could not be said that it was a genuine pre-estimate.

M & J Polymers Limited v Imerys Minerals Limited [2008] EWHC 344 (Comm)

Take or pay clause was deemed a penalty (i.e. a clause which requires the other party to pay for a minimum volume even if they did not order that volume, was declared unenforceable).

It is, however, important to note that in SLAs the service credits (or compensation due for a breach of the SLA) are sometimes not particularly high in view of the contract value as a whole.

Because of this it is unlikely that an organisation will sue a supplier for non-payment of service credits, since the whole point of pre-agreed service credits is to avoid litigation.

The point is that, provided you agree service credits with the supplier which are proportionate to the loss you are likely to suffer (and are not so much more above any loss that you are likely to suffer), then such service credits are likely to be legally enforceable (and are unlikely to be seen as penalty clauses). Also, it will be difficult for the supplier to argue that these service credits are a penalty if it has included these in the SLA and has been advised of the consequences of such penalty clauses by its legal advisers.

Exclusive remedy

The service level credits are your organisation's exclusive remedy. This is because your organisation should have the option to go to court if the standard of service is completely unacceptable (*see Chapter 1*).

Precedence

As discussed, an SLA is a working document and may change from time to time, depending on your organisation's ongoing business needs. However, the provisions of the SLA should not generally override what was agreed in the framework agreement. This is because the provisions of the framework agreement (e.g. payment terms, exit, renewals, intellectual property, etc.) are likely to have been keenly negotiated by a senior management team and lawyers for each party, without the parties expecting these provisions to be overridden by changes to the SLA. If, however, you require specific provisions of the SLA to take precedence over, and override the framework agreement, then this should be done formally via a formal contract variation to the framework agreement, pursuant to the terms of the framework agreement. The terms of the framework agreement will often allow it to be amended if both parties agree to the amendment in writing.

Sweep-up clauses

SLAs can often include sweep-up clauses. These are general blanket clauses which your organisation may try to use to cover a wide variety of obligations.

For example, your organisation might require the supplier to comply with:

- All of your organisation's internal policies.
- All of the regulations to which your organisation is subject (e.g. financial services regulations if your organisation is in this sector).
- All rules, guidelines, codes of practice, regulations and laws that might apply to the provision of the services.

These broad, sweeping clauses might either be objected

to by the supplier or, if not, may go unnoticed until your organisation tries to rely on these in order to cover a particular issue or event.

Generally, it is much better to spell out any particular issues which you wish the supplier to cover, so that the supplier is clear about what it is meant to be doing, and can also 'price in' any such services into its pricing for the services. Although some may say that these sweep-up clauses can assist your organisation if you can get them into your SLA with the supplier, it could be that when you come to rely upon these clauses, there is a dispute with the supplier, since the supplier argues that the services requested were never meant to be included.

Although your organisation may well be able to successfully argue that such services should be included (according to the wording of the relevant sweep-up clauses), this is likely to jeopardise your relationship with the supplier. Further, because your organisation is reliant upon the supplier's ongoing services (and goodwill), any dispute with the supplier is likely to lead to a deterioration in the ongoing relationship which could lead to, amongst other things, a lack of co-operation from your supplier and a deterioration in services provided.

Clause cross referencing

Lots of cross referencing to clauses of the framework agreement (e.g. the IT outsourcing agreement) should be avoided, as otherwise this means that people using the SLA will then need to familiarise themselves with lots of the provisions of the framework agreement, where the framework agreement could be voluminous. This, then, defeats the object of the SLA being a simple, working document that can be used on a day-to- day basis.

Summary

In summary, your organisation should double check that it has considered the clauses which it should, and should not, include above, in order to ensure that the SLA is legally and commercially valid.

The next chapter goes on to cover how your organisation can use an SLA (or elements within it) to influence supplier behaviour, so that it obtains the services which it requires, and that they are provided in the way and manner in which it wants them.

CHAPTER 5: MANAGING THE SUPPLIER

Many organisations think that the SLA should simply list the service levels, the acceptable service level targets, and provide sufficient compensation. However, there is much more to SLAs than this. SLAs also relate to people and the behaviours that the supplier might adopt, rather than being legal documents alone.

SLAs can have the power to:

- Be a deterrent against the supplier providing a poor service.
- Be an incentive for the supplier to provide a better service, or an excellent service.
- Guide the supplier into focusing its time, effort and resources into what the customer believes is really important (rather than the supplier spreading its time and resources thinly over a multitude of tasks, without focusing and prioritising important tasks over less important ones).

Examples of elements to address include:

- The customer considering whether any service level credits have already been priced into the supplier's prices. If so, this means that the SLA may be much less powerful than the customer wishes it to be. If the customer suspects that this has happened, then it may not agree a cap on the total service credits that may be due to it if there are service level target breaches.
- The customer identifying a small number of

service levels (which attract service level credits if they are breached), together with another set of benchmarks, called KPIs (Key Performance Indicators), which the supplier should aim to meet but which do not attract service credits. Although one may say that the supplier will simply not try to achieve KPIs if there are no consequences if it fails to do so (i.e. no service credits payable), they can be useful, at the very least, in showing and directing the supplier as to what is required, and also shaping the services provided.

- Identifying incentivisation schemes, such as: service credit bonuses, which are paid to the supplier for excellent service (or which are set off against any service credits that are due to the customer).
- Asking the supplier if the customer can pay any bonuses (or part of these bonuses) for excellent service directly to supplier staff (rather than being retained by the supplier).
- Sharing cost savings which the supplier thinks about, and which the supplier may assist the customer in achieving.
- Updating the SLA regularly, so that any items which are consistently met by the supplier (such that they are the expected norm) are replaced with items which are not being met by the supplier, or which the customer would like to add, in order to redirect the supplier's efforts, or to reshape the services provided. This reshaping could also be related to different business directions taken by your organisation, or simply the fact that the supplier meeting a pre-defined service level or target might have added value in the past, but now

has much less value, due to your organisation's ongoing and changing requirements. However, the scope which you have to amend the SLA in this way will depend a lot on what options you have negotiated into the SLA. In particular, if changes you require are likely to cost the supplier more to provide, then the supplier will typically then ask for more money to accommodate your requested changes.

- Identifying where action (via action plans) would be a more appropriate remedy than compensation. Since, compensation that is paid does not automatically mean that there is a remedy to the problem complained about.
- Identifying what the supplier may value, and which your organisation can provide to the supplier, in order to foster and build trust and good working relationships.

This may not simply be confined to monetary items but could include, for example, your organisation acting as a reference site for the supplier's potential customers, providing testimonials for the supplier, identifying areas of new work, or engaging in contract extension talks.

Summary

It is important to not simply view the SLA as a legal document, but, instead, to insert provisions into it which help influence supplier behaviour, in order to give your organisation a better service.

The next chapter looks at issues that your organisation should consider when negotiating an SLA.

CHAPTER 6: NEGOTIATING THE SLA

One of the key dangers when negotiating the SLA is that it is treated and dealt with in exactly the same way, in terms of negotiations, as the framework agreement. Often the SLA is drafted by, and then tabled by, one party to the other party.

This first draft of the SLA then often goes through various drafts and revisions before the final SLA, and its wording, is agreed by the parties.

The framework agreement is often heavily negotiated, with a lot of time being spent by lawyers, accountants, consultants, and the senior management teams of both parties, to come to some kind of agreement. Such an agreement will contain numerous clauses with caveats, carve outs, conditions and pre-conditions that each party's lawyers will be heavily involved with.

Having reached agreement on the framework agreement, it is sometimes the case that the parties then move on to the schedules (of which the SLA will often form part).

At this point, the parties may continue to adopt exactly the same approach as with the framework agreement, so that all of the services, service levels and targets are keenly contested and negotiated with lots of provisos and carve outs. The danger here is that rather than being a simple, straightforward working document, the SLA is full of legal jargon and complex provisos which are unintelligible to the project managers and personnel who are intended to operate, implement and manage the SLA and service performance. This can lead to the SLA being disregarded by each party's project managers when operating and reviewing the services.

Alternatively, it is sometimes the case that the parties have spent so much time, energy, cost and resources negotiating the framework agreement that they believe that they have a concluded deal. This means that the feeling is that:

- The parties do not have the energy, appetite and enthusiasm to bring up yet more issues by talking about and formulating a good SLA.
- Time has run out for negotiations, such that there is no real time to put together a good SLA.
- The parties allocate work on the SLA (particularly if it is IT-related) to the 'techies', where the senior management team and lawyers may be reluctant, after spending so much time negotiating the framework agreement, to wade through and check any technical or operational information which makes up the services and service levels.

The danger here is that no SLA, or a very basic SLA, might be put in place. Here, your organisation would not get the full benefit of the SLA and this can leave the supplier without any direction from you, as to the exact services you want and the standards you expect.

Therefore, to try to avoid the problems above, it is a good idea to:

- Treat the SLA with as much importance as the framework agreement.

- Negotiate the SLA at the same time as, and in parallel with, the framework agreement, so that they are agreed at the same time.
- Not leave the SLA as an afterthought.
- Identify the roles that each member of your team will play in negotiating the framework agreement and the SLA. It might be the CIO or IT director that takes control of the SLA, whereas it might be the CEO that leads on the framework agreement, with the CIO and CEO liaising with one another regarding progress on these agreements.

SLA handover

The ideal position is that the people (e.g. project managers) at your organisation that are going to implement the SLA, are at the negotiating table, and have input into the negotiations and preparation. This helps to ensure that those project managers understand the SLA, how it came about, what it is intended to achieve, and have bought into the principles set out in the SLA. This all helps with the smooth implementation of the SLA by those project managers.

However, although it may seem surprising, the project manager or IT manager that is expected to operate, implement and manage the SLA, has frequently not had any involvement in the negotiations relating to the final version of the SLA. This may be because no one has thought about involving the relevant project manager, or that their input or involvement in the negotiation and preparation is viewed as unnecessary.

Sometimes the project manager is simply handed the

SLA to manage, without any real briefing about its structure, how it came about, or any particular results that it is meant to achieve. It might be that, after signature of the SLA, the parties and individuals that negotiated it (e.g. the senior management team, lawyers, consultants and/or accountants) may believe their work is done and simply walk away, so that the SLA document is simply passed to the project manager to get on with.

However, a lot of the work done by the senior management team at your organisation, together with lawyers, consultants, and accountants, in negotiating the framework agreement and SLA with the supplier, can be wasted because the project manager is unaware of:

- The key terms that were fought for in negotiations by your organisation.
- Items which were crucial to your organisation to have in the SLA.
- Particular concessions that your organisation managed to achieve.
- Particular commitments that the supplier made to your organisation.

Although the SLA should be a relatively simple and straightforward document, if the project manager at your organisation does not have all the background to the SLA, then:

- It might be difficult for them to digest all of the provisions and nuances of the SLA.
- The supplier may argue that the project manager has misinterpreted the provisions of the SLA because they were not in the negotiations.

- The project manager at your organisation may be reluctant to keep bothering your senior management team about guidance on the SLA, and therefore may concede on points with the supplier so as to avoid creating issues (which in retrospect they should <u>not</u> have conceded).

Hence, if an SLA is negotiated, then if project managers have not been involved in negotiating the SLA, it is useful to have a written summary prepared by the senior management team, the lawyers or consultants, for the project managers who are going to be operating the SLA, on your organisation's behalf. This, at least, provides some background. Ideally, there would be a presentation as well by the people who negotiated the SLA and framework agreement which highlights what exactly the SLA is meant to do. Further, if someone who was at the negotiations is also involved (in whole or in part) in managing the SLA, then this will mean that there is some continuity between the negotiation of the SLA and the process of implementing the SLA (and will help to avoid project managers disregarding the SLA).

The impact of the IT outsourcing contract

As mentioned, an SLA is likely to form part of a wider deal in the framework agreement (e.g. the IT outsourcing contract). However, clauses of the framework agreement could impact upon what has been agreed in the SLA, and so special care needs to be taken when drafting the SLA, so that clauses in the SLA are not cut across, overridden or watered down by what is said in the framework agreement.

Typical issues to consider which may appear in the framework agreement (and which may impact upon the provisions of the SLA) are included below.

Force majeure clauses

Force majeure clauses in the framework agreement may dictate that the supplier is not liable or responsible under the contract, or the SLA, for any events or matters which are outside its reasonable control. Typically, these force majeure events will include Acts of God, war, flood and fire.

However, lawyers often go further and say that a force majeure event will include other things too, such as strikes, labour disputes, problems with telecommunications, inability to obtain equipment or materials, acts of sub-contractors, and problems with the Internet. However, all of these things are arguably under the control of the supplier (rather than being outside its reasonable control). For example, labour disputes may not occur if the supplier accedes to its labour force's wishes, and so perhaps the exception for labour disputes should be amended to only relate to industry-wide labour disputes which would normally be outside a supplier's reasonable control.

The point here is that your organisation might be entitled to service credits, but then the supplier may argue that its inability to perform was due to a force majeure event of some sort, thereby excluding your organisation's right to be paid service credits. Such an argument may not have been anticipated by your organisation and so it needs to cross check these provisions and their effect between the framework agreement and the SLA.

Limitations of liability

The supplier will probably have limited its liability in the framework agreement to a certain figure, say for example, one million pounds in total. However, an organisation will want to ensure that if it is paid pre-agreed service credits over a period of time, due to the supplier not hitting targets in the SLA, then this should not count towards the supplier's overall cap on liability. For example, if the cap is one million pounds and the supplier pays £150,000 in service credits over the period of a contract, then if your organisation suddenly has a big claim against the supplier, it does not want to have the supplier argue that the supplier's cap is actually £850,000 (since £150,000 has already been paid in service credits).

Suspension

A lot of framework agreements will enable the supplier to suspend the provision of services in certain circumstances, pending resolution of the issue that has triggered the suspension. Typically, this may be in relation to payment (i.e. the supplier is entitled to suspend services upon reasonable notice, if it is not paid on time). However, such a clause may have been expanded so that services can be suspended to cater for issues such as scheduled maintenance work, upgrade work, or investigation of any problems which threaten to make a major impact upon the system. However, this suspension could mean that services are not subject to service credits during such a suspension, or that such down time will not be taken into account in the calculation of service credits. Hence, the SLA needs to address this point directly.

Set-off

The set-off provisions of a framework agreement may allow one party to set off monies that it is owed by another party, against monies which it owes that party. The point here is that an organisation will want to know if it can set off monies which it is owed in service credits, against any payments due to the supplier (rather than having to pay the supplier in full and then try to claim back service credits later on). This point, and what should happen here, should be covered in the framework agreement and/or SLA. Normally, the parties will agree that neither party can set off monies owed to it against monies payable by it, unless the other party agrees to this at the time.

Summary

When negotiating an SLA, it is important that:

- You see this as part of the whole process of negotiating a wider deal (and not simply tag the negotiation of the SLA on to the end of the deal).
- The SLA is negotiated, so that its provisions do not cut across the provisions of the framework agreement (and *vice versa*).

CHAPTER 7: PUTTING THE SLA INTO ACTION

Changes

The framework agreement will last for a number of years, and so it is inevitable that the services required may need to change.

Some organisations may be reluctant to raise the need for changes with the supplier because they may believe that this might be seen by the supplier as an opportunity to revisit and review prices (upwards). However, your organisation may be unable to avoid these discussions with the supplier if changes are essential. Ideally, you will have considered and incorporated many of the anticipated changes into your SLA, so that if these changes do happen, then they can be dealt with as set out in the SLA.

If not, then additional goods and/or services, or changes to goods and/or services, are likely to cost more (or you might want to reduce services but the supplier may insist that the same prices are payable, with no reduction in price for reduction in services).

In order to get a better deal, or to get the supplier to allow you to make changes to the deal, you may need to encourage the supplier to agree to the deal changes that you want by offering the supplier incentives, such as:

- Contract extension.
- More service orders, either from your organisation, or other associated organisations.
- Better payment terms for the supplier, so it gets

paid earlier than it otherwise might do under the original contract.

- Using the supplier in preference to other suppliers that your organisation may be using.
- Allowing your supplier to use your IT systems as a reference site for potential new customers, to help show these potential new customers what the supplier has done for your organisation.
- Providing testimonials or references for the supplier regarding any good work that it has done for your organisation.

Increased costs

Increased costs will be a normal factor to take into account as services are provided, since it often becomes clear to organisations that different services, or additional services, are required from time to time.

Again, by keeping communication channels open with the supplier via meetings and ongoing talks, your organisation may be able to negotiate a change in the landscape of the services for the same cost. Your organisation may also discuss where the supplier can see cost efficiencies where services can be streamlined.

For example, if certain services are particularly expensive for the supplier to provide, then you may:

- Allow the supplier to reduce some of these in exchange for charging you less.
- Agree to relax the service level targets (particularly if you subsequently realise that such high targets are not really necessary).
- Reduce the amount or number of service credits

payable (in return for lower charges), particularly if the service credits payable are nominal, or if they have not been paid because the service has been satisfactory.

Poor performance

It is important to understand why your supplier might not be meeting targets that have been set out in the SLA. If you can identify the root causes of poor performance, then you might be able to put in measures to tackle these root causes early on. If you fail to identify these root causes and let them fester, then it may well be that services deteriorate further, leading to major problems later on.

Your organisation should ask itself if any poor performance is because:

- Service credits have already been priced into the contract price, and so providing the service to a lower standard, is a price worth paying for by the supplier. If the amount of service credits payable increases over time, then you might ask the supplier why this is, in order to identify what the root cause might be.
- The supplier has more lucrative contracts, so that your contract is of low priority (or your contract has become low priority for the supplier over time, as the supplier has become more successful or has obtained more customers, or has devoted more of its time to new customers and new business). If this is the case, then you might not renew the contract with this supplier.
- The supplier is stretched, in that it does not have

the staff and resources to service your contract properly.

- Your contract has been so keenly negotiated that the only way the supplier can make any money from it, is to reduce the amount of staff and resources it dedicates to the service.
- The supplier has committed to higher standards than it can actually achieve, in order to win the contract with your organisation.

Whatever the reason, once the root causes of poor supplier performance are fully understood by your organisation, you can then begin to address this with the supplier, or devise alternative strategies in order to counter this poor performance. This could include not renewing the contract, thinking about appointing a new supplier, incentivising your existing supplier, or renegotiating the SLA so that it is mutually beneficial for both your organisation and the supplier.

Ending the SLA

The SLA will typically end at the same time that the framework agreement is terminated or expires (and is often subject to the termination provisions in the framework agreement, for services such as the main IT outsourcing agreement).

However, the SLA may have a 'wind down' or 'run off' period built into it, so that the framework agreement may be terminated on a particular day, but then there is, say, a three-month run-off period, so that the services can be ended in an orderly fashion and/or can be transferred over to either your organisation's own in-house department, or an alternative third party supplier.

The SLA should contain various provisions regarding exit or 'run-off', including keeping the service in 'standstill' mode, so it simply continues normally (i.e. obliging the supplier to not make any major changes to the services during the run- off period, not to start any new projects, and/or not to add staff to, or remove staff from, the team that is delivering the services, unless this is with your consent).

Note that under TUPE (the Transfer of Undertakings (Protection of Employment) Regulations 2006) in the UK[4], you may be obliged to become the employer of the supplier's pool of employees whose job entailed being dedicated to providing the services to your organisation. One issue here is that you would not want the supplier to transfer employees out of this pool just before the end of the contract and replace them with poor employees, thereby ensuring that the poor employees were the ones that transferred over to your organisation at the end of the contract.

Other issues that need to be considered and agreed in the framework agreement and/or SLA regarding the end of a contract include:

- Which services you expect to be maintained until termination and which services you expect to cease immediately.
- The manner in which services will cease or be

---

4 Further information about TUPE is currently available at
www.acas.org.uk/index.aspx?articleid=1655.

reduced.

- Any cost implications of the 'run-off' period (for example, will you pay less for reduced services and/or will you pay extra for any extra work required in winding down the relevant services?).
- A complete and accurate report on the up-to-date position regarding the services, in terms of who they are provided by, any problems with the services, any ongoing projects, and any other issues that might affect the services.

Summary

When managing an SLA your organisation will need to be fully aware of how its service requirements change over time and how this will affect the SLA.

In addition, if your service requirements have changed over time, then this will affect any exit plan or run-off period.

Outlined below are the key questions raised in each of the chapters.

| **Chapter 1** | Why do you need an SLA?

Where do SLAs fit into the document structure?

What are service levels, service level targets, and service level credits?

What are the benefits of SLAs? |
|---|---|

Chapter 2	Where do SLAs go wrong?
	What should you be aware of regarding using lawyers to prepare your SLA?
Chapter 3	Building the foundation for the SLA.
	What preparation work can you do before preparing the SLA?
Chapter 4	Drafting the SLA and key clauses.
	What are the key clauses that you should/should not include in the SLA?
Chapter 5	Managing the supplier.
	What elements influence supplier behaviour?
Chapter 6	What key elements must be considered when drafting your SLA?
	How can the framework agreement affect the SLA?
Chapter 7	How can your organisation best manage the SLA?
	How can your organisation understand how problems have arisen?
	What should your organisation be considering prior to ending the SLA?

The framework agreement and SLA provide the important bridge between you, the customer, and your supplier.

It is vital that your framework agreement and SLA are drafted properly, and that they dovetail properly with one another. The SLA matters because your organisation can quickly become highly dependent upon your IT supplier, and the framework agreement (including the SLA) is the framework within which you can negotiate changes, in a way that will help to minimise disruption, additional costs and/or delays.

Ending an SLA can be difficult, but the process can be made manageable, as long as the framework agreement and SLA contain a comprehensive exit plan to ensure a smooth transition of services back to your organisation, or to a replacement IT supplier.

Finally, you will know only too well that good IT is the backbone of a successful organisation. If you decide that managing your own IT function is not your core business (as many medium to large organisations do), and that the way forward is to outsource the function, then it is important to identify early on what sort of expert legal and other advice you might wish to access and obtain – in order to ensure that the process goes smoothly and you do not store up unexpected problems (or costs) for the future.

ITG RESOURCES

IT Governance Ltd sources, creates and delivers products and services to meet the real-world, evolving IT governance needs of today's organisations, directors, managers and practitioners. The ITG website (*www.itgovernance.co.uk*) is the international one-stop- shop for corporate and IT governance information, advice, guidance, books, tools, training and consultancy.

www.itgovernance.co.uk/sla.aspx is the information page on our website for our service level agreement resources.

Other Websites

Books and tools published by IT Governance Publishing (ITGP) are available from all business booksellers and are also immediately available from the following websites:

www.itgovernance.co.uk/catalog/355 provides information and online purchasing facilities for every currently available book published by ITGP.

www.itgovernanceusa.com is a US$-based website that delivers the full range of IT Governance products to North America, and ships from within the continental US.

www.itgovernanceasia.com provides a selected range of ITGP products specifically for customers in South Asia.

www.27001.com is the IT Governance Ltd website that deals specifically with information security management, and ships from within the continental US.

Pocket Guides

For full details of the entire range of pocket guides, simply follow the links at *www.itgovernance.co.uk/publishing.aspx.*

Toolkits

ITG's unique range of toolkits includes the IT Governance Framework Toolkit, which contains all the tools and guidance that you will need in order to develop and implement an appropriate IT governance framework for your organisation. Full details can be found at *www.itgovernance.co.uk/ products/519.*

For a free paper on how to use the proprietary Calder-Moir IT Governance Framework, and for a free trial version of the toolkit, see *www.itgovernance.co.uk/calder_moir.aspx.*

There is also a wide range of toolkits to simplify implementation of management systems, such as an ISO/IEC 27001 ISMS or a BS25999 BCMS, and these can all be viewed and purchased online at: *www.itgovernance.co.uk/catalog/1.*

Best Practice Reports

ITG's range of Best Practice Reports is now at *www.itgovernance.co.uk/best-practice-reports.aspx.* These offer you essential, pertinent, expertly researched information on an increasing number of key issues including Web 2.0 and Green IT.

Training and Consultancy

IT Governance also offers training and consultancy services across the entire spectrum of disciplines in the information governance arena. Details of training courses can be accessed at *www.itgovernance.co.uk/training.aspx* and descriptions of our consultancy services can be found at *www.itgovernance.co.uk/consulting.aspx*. Why not contact us to see how we could help you and your organisation?

Newsletter

IT governance is one of the hottest topics in business today, not least because it is also the fastest moving, so what better way to keep up than by subscribing to ITG's free monthly newsletter Sentinel? It provides monthly updates and resources across the whole spectrum of IT governance subject matter, including risk management, information security, ITIL and IT service management, project governance, compliance and so much more. Subscribe for your free copy at:
www.itgovernance.co.uk/newsletter.aspx

Lightning Source UK Ltd.
Milton Keynes UK
UKOW04f0144060716

277729UK00016B/351/P